Prospecting Your Way to Sales Success

Prospecting Your Way to Sales Success

HOW TO FIND
NEW BUSINESS BY PHONE

Bill Good

CHARLES SCRIBNER'S SONS / NEW YORK

Charles Scribner's Sons
Macmillan Publishing Company
866 Third Avenue, New York, NY 10022
Collier Macmillan Canada, Inc.

Library of Congress Cataloging-in-Publication Data

Good, Bill.
    Prospecing your way to sales sucess.

    Includes index.
    1. Selling   2. Telephone selling.   I. Title
HF5438.25.G65   1986   658.8'5   86-6470
ISBN 0-684-18620-9

Macmillan books are available at special discounts for bulk purchases
for sales promotions, premiums, fund-raising, or educational use.
For details, contact:
                Special Sales Director
                Macmillan Publishing Company
                866 Third Avenue
                New York, NY 10022

10 9 8 7 6 5

    Designed by Marek Antoniak

Printed in the United States of America

*To all the countless millions
of salespeople who would
rather stand in a cold shower
ripping up $100 bills
than make cold prospecting calls*

Contents

Acknowledgments

Looking back, there were many who helped.

My Mom and Dad, my Mom for the joy of learning, my Dad for the joy of life.

Herb Hazelman, my band director at Greensboro Senior High. Before excellence was a fad, he demanded it. And in the process of teaching music, he taught so much more.

Mrs. Weaver and Mrs. Winchester, two ninth grade teachers who made a difference, and who still do.

My wife Joava. After months of preparation, I was ready to start my business, but had less than a thousand dollars to live on. Too risky. So I told her I was going to wait. She took me on a walk around the block. She asked, "What's the worst that could happen?" I replied, "We'd go broke, the creditors would get the furniture and car, and we would have to go on welfare?" "Do you think you could ever work again?" she wanted to know. "Sure," I said. "A good salesman can always work." "So what are you going to do?" "I'm going to go for it." Without that nudge, I might not have done it. Life since would not have been as much fun.

Howard Shenson, President of Howard L. Shenson, Inc. When I met Howard in 1977 he was "big time" in the seminars business. I was trying to figure out how to get started. I called and asked him for help. He gave a lot. And if I have made a success at it, he pointed the way.

Barry Weiner, President of Homeowners Marketing Service. When I didn't have the money to promote my first seminar, he let me slip a brochure into his own customer mailing and didn't charge me for it.

The late L. Ron Hubbard. Beneath the controversy, such wisdom. Anyone who is serious at all about improving their communication and organizational skills will study the works of this giant.

And of course, my staff at Telephone Marketing, Inc.

Prospecting Your Way to Sales Success

Introduction

This book is about one thing and one thing only—SALES PROS-PECTING. In it I'll show you how to find more and better prospects. For you this means only two things: more sales and more M O N E Y.

So the goal of this book, then, is to help you make more sales and more money by improving the quantity and quality of your prospects. Whatever your level of selling skill, if you have more and better prospects, you will make more sales and more M O N E Y.

The main tool we'll use in our search for prospects will be the telephone. It's faster and, properly used, far more effective than wearing out shoe leather trudging door-to-door or running up the boss's postage bill.

But there is a problem with the phone. Most salespeople would rather do almost anything than prospect by phone, and indeed some get to the point where they believe the phone weighs five hundred pounds or may even be one of the new models that only accept incoming calls. If this describes you at all, you've got the right book, because I'm going to show you how to enjoy prospecting more. (You may be among those who will never like prospecting. Follow my methods, and I promise you will SUFFER LESS.)

WHO SHOULD READ THIS BOOK?

Notice I said "Who should read this book?" I naturally think everyone should buy one. But once you've bought it, don't read it unless you're "qualified." By "qualified," I mean:

- You don't like prospecting and would prefer dental drilling or at least would prefer to do something else. If you like it, chances are you're good at it. And unless you particularly want to get better at it, after you've bought the book, just pass it along to a friend.

- You need more prospects. If you have all the prospective customers you need, you obviously don't have to study up on how to get more.

- You can find "enough" prospect names with phone numbers.

To see if you're qualified to read this book, we need to spend a little time on the question "Can you get enough names?" That is, are there enough prospective customers out there for your product or service?

Can You Get Enough Names?

The answer to the question "Are there enough?" is, ultimately, a matter of numbers. How many is "enough"?

The rule of thumb I work with is "several hundred." Depending on your market, to begin a profitable telephone-based prospecting campaign, you need to be able to identify several hundred potential buyers.

Let's take an example where there are *not* enough. Let's say you are an account executive for a creative advertising house specializing in print ads for motion pictures. You might have as few as twenty-five to thirty prospects. These would be motion picture studios. That's twenty-five or thirty in the whole United States! So you couldn't afford to waste a single one. You have an extremely limited market, and some prospecting approach would have to be followed other than the one I will outline in this book. My method *does allow* for waste and mistakes.

Most likely, your method for approaching an extremely limited market would have to be based on some version of the "old boy" network. Your success will depend upon who you know and how well you know them.

By way of contrast, let's take a look at some markets that clearly lend themselves to a telephone-prospecting campaign:

- Residential Real Estate: Sixteen percent of the American population move each year, according to a 1983 Bureau of the Census study. With this many people on the move, the residential real estate market is clearly large enough to support a telephone-prospecting campaign.

- Commercial Real Estate: With all the change, expansion, and contraction of new businesses being formed and old businesses being bought, sold, and going bankrupt, there is a constant need for commercial offices and buildings. In any of the major metropolitan markets, the telephone is the prospecting method of choice.

- Securities Industry: My company, Telephone Marketing, Inc., has trained tens of thousands of stockbrokers since 1980, and any hour of the day, someone I have trained can pick up the phone and find two to four *good prospects* in that single hour!

- Insurance: One out of nine adults in the United States will buy life insurance this year. In virtually every state, anyone with a driver's license is required by law to have automobile insurance.

- Dentistry: Not too long ago I read an article that said forty-five percent of the population does not have a regular dentist. I applied the principles I'll be teaching you to that market and created a low-key prospecting campaign that generated eighty-two new patients in the first month for our "test dentist." His previous record was thirty-five new patients in a single month.

- Home Repair, Home Improvement, and Automobile Sales: These quite obviously lend themselves to a telephone-prospecting campaign. What about all those car salesmen you see waiting in line at the dealership for a prospect to come in the front door? If I were running those dealerships, there wouldn't be a line of salespeople. They would all be on the phones, with only one person waiting.

- Banking: This is a natural in today's new deregulated business climate. Computer sales personnel, facing an increasingly competitive market, can't wait for those incoming calls anymore. They've got to get out and beat the bush.

- Office equipment and supplies?: Obviously.

- Books, educational materials, and instruction of any kind can be prospected for by phone. As a matter of fact, I have a forty-dollar University of North Carolina Alumni Association Directory sitting on my bookshelf as the result of a talented, pleasant saleswoman.

Go through any issue of a daily newspaper, and you'll see the tremendous application telephone prospecting can have for finding customers. Here are some applications I got by going through one issue of one paper:

Season tickets to sporting events

Furniture

Telephone campaigns to credit card holders at department stores

Temporary employment agencies

Executive placement services

Classified ad sales

Display ad sales for newspapers

Book sales

New members for churches

Prepaid funeral services

Newspaper subscriptions

Family portraits

Chimney cleaning

Photocopiers

If your product or service fits or resembles any of these categories, read on!

WHO SHOULDN'T READ THIS BOOK

This book is not for superstars or those who aspire to superstar status. A superstar is a "natural" salesperson. Occasionally such people write books, and a typical book jacket will read: "Roland Macho was the first million-dollar salesman ever by age thirteen. By fifteen, he had purchased his own insurance agency and was well on his way to his second million. Now he shares his secrets with you."

Or: "By age eight, Joanne Macha had sold more lemonade at her stand at the corner of 8th and Grand than has ever been sold in the history of the world. By age eleven, she had 11,467 people in her direct marketing group, and is listed in the *Guinness Book of Records* as the most successful child since Mozart. You too can learn the secrets of MILLION DOLLAR selling by reading her book."

These people are superstars, and this book is not for them. Nor is it for people who are on a fast track to achieve superstar status.

The typical superstar can sell "ice to Eskimos" and frankly can do things that you and I could never do, and possibly would not do even if we could.

Three Steps to Success

Notice I include myself in that category of nonsuperstars. As a salesman, I'm good. I can sell most any decent product. But I am not one of those who can sell something to someone who doesn't want it. I concentrate on finding people who need what I've got and then get them excited about it. If you follow this approach, closing the sale is no big deal.

My own abilities to practice what I will preach to you in this book have brought me and my company from nowhere to the front page of the *Wall Street Journal;* to guest appearances on the most highly rated business radio talk show in the country; to training accounts with many of the country's major stock brokerage firms, insurance companies, and real estate firms; to speaking engagements in England, Brazil, and Puerto Rico; to prime time TV appearances; to a monthly column in *Registered Representative,* the major trade magazine in the securities industry; and to a keynote address before the Securities Industry Association in Philadelphia.

To succeed in sales, as I have done, you only need to do three things:

1. Find a product or service you like, know, and believe in and which people need and want.

2. Develop a way to find those who want it and can afford it NOW!

3. Have a well-designed sales presentation and two or three different closes.

In this book, we'll be concentrating on Step Number 2: how to develop a way to find those who want it and can afford it NOW! As you get into the book, you'll see that we'll really just be talking common sense methods. You'll wonder why no one ever taught them to you before.

The origin of these ideas goes back to my first selling job, selling dictionaries door-to-door for Southwest Publishing Company one summer while I was in college. Not only was I not a superstar, but I found the entire process of sales so frightening that I used to get sick every morning at the very thought of being rejected.

I can recall hours spent and gallons of gas wasted while I drove around looking for the perfect house—the one that contained a buyer, someone who would welcome my approach, who needed my dictionary, and who could afford the ten dollars to buy it.

Admittedly, the idea that I could identify a guaranteed buyer by looking at the outside of a house was flaky at best. But the germ of the idea—that there ought to be a way to find *good* prospects —was correct. Frankly, this book is proof that my misguided search for the perfect house actually paid off. Of course, I never did learn how to identify the perfect house merely by looking at it. But I guessed then, and I know now, that there had to be a better way to find business than talking to everyone on the block.

I figured that there were indeed people somewhere who needed what I had to offer. The trick was simply to find them. The answer, ultimately, was simple. Not necessarily easy. Just simple.

WHAT YOU WILL LEARN

To achieve the goal of this book—to improve your sales and commission by improving the quantity and quality of your prospects—you'll need to know some things you don't know now. Among other things, I'll show you:

- How to become the "rejector," not the "rejectee." We'll end the pain of prospecting at a single stroke.

- How to develop lists of qualified prospects who are likely to be interested in your product or service and want it NOW.

- How to deal with secretaries or other intervening parties. If your blood pressure rises at the thought of being put on hold by just one more secretary, you're in for a treat. Any one of the six methods I'll show you will enormously improve your ability to contact your prospect.

- How to design a prospecting call that can help you find out if a particular prospect is right for your business NOW.

- How to make more calls than you ever dreamed possible. Since the birth of business, sales trainers have preached that "sales is a numbers" game. I'm going to show you how to make the hidden truth in the numbers game work for you, not against you.

A WARNING

The methods I will outline are simple. But they require some hard work, the old-fashioned kind.

Not pressure.

Nor force.

Just hard work.

So if you are browsing through the introduction of this book before buying it and if it looks like something that might benefit you, go ahead. It will make your life in sales easier and more enjoyable. And you'll certainly enjoy more good prospects than you have ever dreamed possible.

So did you want one book or two?

Cash or check?

1

Prospecting:
The Old School
versus the New School

You came into sales to sell, and it's not working out that way.

Perhaps you wanted to be a stockbroker and help people make their fortune (as well as your own, of course). You didn't dream that most of your time would be spent punching out phone calls in an endless search for people with money. And worse, you had no idea that people wouldn't welcome your call. After all, you have ideas that should help people get a better return on their money than they now enjoy.

Or perhaps you are in real estate. You wanted to help people find new homes, not spend hours sitting at an open house that no one attends, or walking door-to-door to meet the neighbors. And just last week, a piece of bone and hair that resembled a dog scared you half to death as it lunged at you from under a shrub.

Or you sell life insurance. You know that if you can help one or two families each week protect their assets and estates, provide for their children and families, that you can make a very good living in the process.

You found out in a hurry, of course, that most people really don't want to talk to a life insurance agent. But not even in your most pessimistic brooding about your future did you realize it could be as bad as it really is.

The problem was really driven home to you at the Christmas party at the company where your wife works. She had warned you not to talk business, but in the back of your mind, you had an idea that people would at least want to know about some of the new life insurance products on the market.

Drink in hand, you coolly bided your time, and as expected, someone asked what you do for a living.

You said, "I'm a life insurance agent."

You might as well have said, "I'm a mentally disordered sex offender currently under psychiatric care." The room couldn't have emptied out any faster.

Now certainly you didn't come into sales to frighten or offend people.

THE PROBLEM WITH SALES IS PROSPECTING!

Where did all the prospects go? Are there just too many salespeople? Or did something happen to scare them off?

Worse, the longer you've been in sales, the more you hate prospecting. Why? They turn you down, reject you. And because they reject you and because prospects are so hard to come by, you try harder and harder. And the harder you try, the more scared they get.

It's interesting that the major problem in sales is not really a problem with sales. It's a *prospecting* problem.

And that problem is: scarcity. Most salespeople act as if there are too few good prospects.

The reason you are holding this book is that *you don't have enough prospects.* If you had all you could handle, you certainly wouldn't be looking at a book on prospecting. Yes, I am very well aware that ninety-nine percent of the salespeople in this country believe that rejection is THE PROBLEM. But that's not it. If you *really believed* that there were enough prospects for you, would you care if some jerk turned you down?

But since you, and most other salespeople believe—consciously or subconsciously—that prospects are scarce, then rejection threatens survival. And that hurts.

So rejection is not the problem in sales. Nor is it closing, a lack of product or service knowledge, too high a price, the "competition," or poor company advertising.

It's scarcity of prospects. But we live in a country of 235 million people. How can prospects be scarce?

Julius Caesar said, "The fault, dear Brutus, is not in our stars but in ourselves, that we are underlings."

I say, "The fault for our scarcity of prospects lies not in the market, but in our method." And that method is one I'll call the Old School.

THE OLD SCHOOL STYLE OF SELLING

Every sales trainer I ever had, plus all that I've read, have focused on overcoming objections and on closing. J. Douglas Edwards, perhaps the best of what I call the Old School trainers, preached that "half of your sales will be made after the prospect has said 'No' six times." Mona Ling, a prominent trainer in the insurance industry, promotes "tested answers" to life insurance objections. A flyer promoting a set of cassette tapes came across my desk recently featuring a photo of the trainer and the back end of his car. His "vanity" license plate said "CLOSER."

This concentration on closing and overcoming objections has defined a lifestyle for countless millions of salespeople. In order to understand fully the fact that this is not another book in that tradition, I do think we should spend a few minutes highlighting the Old School. Then you will understand what my system *isn't*.

Old School Teachings

If you have been around sales more than one day, I am certain you have heard one or more versions of the three principles summarized below. I personally have no idea where I first heard them and don't know if anyone should be given credit, or blame, as the case may be. At any rate, here are the philosophical foundations for the Old School.

- All buyers are liars.
- Don't believe the prospect until he or she has said no three, six, twelve, or twenty-seven times.
- Every "No" gets you that much closer to a "Yes."

As you can well imagine, if you believe these principles, they will affect the way you live your life. If you sell insurance, when the prospect says no, you will press ahead anyway thinking you are that much closer to a yes. If you are a stockbroker and the prospect tells you he or she doesn't have any money now, you won't believe him or her but will charge forward anyway, ruining the prospect's evening and your own when the prospect tells you which anatomical portion should receive your phone.

Most Old School salespeople, consciously or otherwise, will believe and act as if there were a war between buyer and seller and that your job as seller is to win! "We Shall Overcome" was not just the theme song of the civil rights movement. It's a song the "sales movement" has been singing for generations. It's one reason your call isn't always welcome. Too many generations of prospects have been overcome.

Applying Old School Principles

If you work in insurance, real estate, most financial services (except, of course, where my company does the training!), appliances, automobiles, or just about anything else, you have most likely been trained in the Old School *if you have had any training at all.*

Let's assume, for the sake of argument, that you are a salesman in one of the financial services companies. Perhaps you sell stocks and bonds. As I am sure you will recognize, the yarn I'm going to spin for you is all too typical. If you don't recognize yourself as the key player, I'm sure you know someone that this applies to directly.

So let's assume you are fairly new in the business, and your branch manager or sales manager has made it perfectly clear that you are expected to cold call (that is, phone someone to whom you've never spoken before) at least five hours a day and probably a couple of evenings each week. On your part, you would much rather wait for someone to call you or at least be provided with twenty or thirty direct mail leads each week.

But—as you find out to your dismay—it doesn't work that way. So you decide to take the plunge one evening when no one is in the office. You sit down at your phone and start calling. Before long, you get Dr. Jones on the phone.

Now you happen to have heard that Dr. Jones has a $300,000

annual income, lives in a $600,000 home, and that he and his wife drive his and hers Mercedeses. So he would, of course, be a highly desirable customer.

Here goes the usual conversation:

YOU: *Ring, ring.*

DR. JONES: Hello.

YOU: May I speak with Dr. Jones, please?

DR. JONES: Speaking.

YOU: Dr. Jones, this is Fred Smithers with Beam of Light Financial Services.

DR. JONES: (Interrupting). Excuse me but I am really not interested.

Before continuing with this now classic conversation, let's review your Old School training.

First of all, you will undoubtedly have been trained to persist. In sales school, you will probably have heard countless anecdotes about how various superstar salespeople have persisted and triumphantly returned with the prized order.

Plus, your sales manager or other brokers will have surely relayed some or all of these Old School gems of wisdom:

- "No is just a stepping stone on the way to Yes."
- "The more No's you get the closer you are to a Yes."
- "No is simply a misunderstanding on the part of the prospect and it is just a way of saying that he or she requires additional information."

With these philosophical pearls jangling loose in your purse or pocket, let's pick up again with your conversation with Dr. Jones, who was saying . . .

DR. JONES: I am really not interested.

YOU: Of course you're not interested. If you had been interested, you would have called me, right?

DR. JONES: (angrily) I guess I would, but I didn't. So what
               does that tell you?

YOU: I understand you are not interested, Doctor. But
               let me just ask you this. What are you not inter-
               ested in?

DR. JONES: I'm not interested in you. I'm not interested in
               Beam of Light Financial Services. But I'm very
               interested in my dinner and besides I'm busy.

YOU: I understand you're busy. I find that most of my
               clients are busy and it's for that reason that . . .

DR. JONES: *Click. Dial tone.*

YOU: Sigh. (Addressing room at large.) I wonder what
               I did wrong?

From the Old School point of view, you certainly must have
done something wrong. Weakness? Wimpy tone in voice? Failure
to persist? Insufficient goal orientation? Bad phone breath?

Sadly, you recall the words of Old School trainer, J. Douglas
Edwards, who said that half of your sales would be made after the
prospect has said no six times. So sitting there with a long face and
with a fly buzzing obnoxiously about the pizza crust on the table,
you reflect on the magic number 6.

"If only," you say to the fly, "I could have gotten Dr. Jones to
say 'No' six times, I might have gotten his account. But," you say
to the coffee cup with bits of creamer curdling on the surface,
"Rome wasn't built in a day."

And so you grind through another eight or twelve calls and not
one sale or appointment do you get. At the end of an hour, you
feel as if you have been passed back and forth through a tree
shredder. You're tired and discouraged.

Walking toward the door, you make a face at Dr. Jones's prospect card, which you have taped to your phone to remind yourself
to call him tomorrow and grind a few more no's out of him.

As you lock up, a terrible thought strikes. There was that video
tape you saw in training. What was it the trainer said? Was it,

"Don't believe the prospect until he has said 'No' twenty-seven times"? It couldn't have been!

Poor you. You couldn't even get Dr. Jones to say it six times.

What a Way to Make a Living!

Now I submit to you that the Old School *is* one hell of a way to make a living. If you happen to be brand new to sales and think I exaggerate that people are trained this way, just pick up any other sales book or attend any sales meeting anywhere. (Definite exception: sales organizations that have had my training.)

If you would like to conduct your own tests of Old School methods, by all means verify the following:

- Try the Old School method for anywhere from one hour to one month. You may grow to hate sales.

- Call up some people and tell them you're a life insurance agent. Talk about rejection! The life insurance industry, as far as I am concerned, is now reaping the harvest of forty years of Old School selling. After all, life insurance agents are trained to believe that if a prospect can generate a pulse, they are immediate prospects for an additional $100 million in whole life.

I hope you do understand that the Old School *does work*—for some people. But these are folks who can leap out of bed each morning, gobble a bowl of rusty nails, and then lunge at the jugular of the nearest prospect. Many average, decent human beings who would like to earn a living in sales *can't live that way!*

So the Old School definitely has two sets of problems:

1) It's very hard on the salesperson. If you don't already hate prospecting, you probably will—if you stick to Old School methods.

2) It is very hard on prospects. Why do you think the room empties out when a life insurance agent introduces himself? It's not the product. People buy it every day. It's the sales method. After decades of nail-pulling sales methods, people have finally come to believe that a session with a life insurance agent will be unpleasant. And so it is.

But lest you think that this school of sales is entirely without redeeming social value, it did serve its purpose. Undoubtedly it came of age in an era in which the old-time peddler could not make more than one call per day. And in the old days, if you didn't sell on that one call, you didn't eat.

Today we live in an entirely different era in sales. Instead of being limited to one call per day, or one per week, the salesperson can cover more time by phone in a hour than the old-time salesperson could cover in a week, or even a month.

So this book is most definitely not about this Old School style of selling.

It's about what I'll call the New School.

THE NEW SCHOOL

The system of prospecting I'm going to outline to you relies upon two very basic assumptions:

(1) There are enough prospects in your market area who are *interested and qualified today* to make it worthwhile to go look for them and to ignore the rest.

By "interested," I mean INTERESTED. Ask a child, "Are you interested in ice cream?" The child's "yes" is the one I'm talking about. Ask the child, "Are you interested in going into the backyard and weeding the garden?" That "no" is the one Old School salespeople grind away on in their misguided efforts to convince the child there is some remote benefit in weeding the garden.

By "qualified" I mean "has capability to buy NOW."

As I pointed out in the Introduction, you do need at least several hundred prospect names. I guarantee you that unless you have an extremely limited market, you can develop a way to simply look for those who are interested and qualified NOW. No problem.

(2) Not all "buyers are liars." In fact, we'll assume the opposite, that buyers tend to be truth tellers.

The old statement, "buyers are liars," is the fundamental assumption on which the Old School is based. The Old School believes that if someone tells you they're not interested, what they really mean is, "I need some additional information."

Or when the buyers tell you, "I don't have any money," what they really mean is, "I don't have any money for that idea, but if you come up with another idea, of course I could raise the money."

I call this "translating English into English." And of course it assumes the prospect doesn't know his or her own mind or is spinning a lie.

Frankly, when you treat people as if they are lying or don't know their own mind, don't be surprised if they don't respond well to your sales message. Undoubtedly, there are many people out there who will lie to you, who will create a smoke screen to tell you they're not interested when they are, and who will rely on other subterfuge to lead you off the trail. Yes, their lies and smoke screens can be penetrated by Old School selling. My question to you is: Do you want a customer list full of liars?

You can build a selling system on one of two assumptions. You can assume, along with the prophets of the Old School, that many buyers are indeed liars. If you make that assumption, you must follow it with all of the various techniques to overcome opposition. You must be prepared to suffer endless rejection. And you must continue the endless process of translating English into English. Or, you can shed the Old School and join the New School and make life almost infinitely easier.

As a practitioner of the New School, instead of grinding away when a prospect says, "I'm not interested," you politely say, "Thankyouverymuch." And then you call the next prospect on your list. You are very literally looking for someone who is interested and qualified now.

So—let's leave the Old School and go in search of the New School.

2

Pick the Cherries Not the Pits: Applying the Principles of the New School

Now that I've given the Old School a blow to the head, I had better offer something in its place. And that's what I am going to do in this chapter. Indeed, the remainder of this book is designed to replace that tired, worn-out way of doing business.

PROSPECTING

Frequently in my training seminars I ask all the trainees in the room to close their eyes. I then say, "Create a picture in your mind of a prospector." When I see they have done that, I then ask them to open their eyes and tell me what they saw. Most people report seeing an old man with a mule, a pick on his shoulder, and a big pack on the back of the mule. Well, we're going to talk about prospecting in exactly the same sense as the old gold prospector.

A decent dictionary definition of the term prospecting is: "the act of searching for something of value." And that is exactly what the old gold prospector did.

Once gold was discovered in California, people came by the millions. They came to California because gold had been found in California. They didn't stop in Fort Lauderdale nor detour through Rio de Janeiro or Easter Island. They were heading for gold rush country!

Once they got there, they would look for certain geological signs that gold might be found in one spot rather than another. Among the things they looked for were deposits of black sand, a heavy iron-based sand. If there was any gold around, it would be mixed in with that sand.

Once the old prospector staked his claim, he would then shovel the sand into his gold pan, and from that point on his primary interest was getting rid of the dirt.

Gold prospecting *was and is primarily the act of discarding that which is not gold.* The prospector gets rid of such things as dirt, grit, gravel, mud, and twigs. And assuming there is gold in his sample to begin with, the more "nongold" he discards, the more gold he finds.

So if the New School has historical roots, they are in the California goldfields, not with the old-time peddler. In New School prospecting, the first effort is: DISQUALIFY NONBUYERS.

The Old School sales trainer counsels various techniques that enable the sales person to hang onto anyone who will speak with him or her. But the New School prospector says, "If it don't glitter, it's dirt and out it goes."

So from the New School point of view, let's rerun the phone call you made to Dr. Jones:

YOU: *Ring, ring.*

DR. JONES: Hello.

YOU: May I speak with Dr. Jones, please?

DR. JONES: Speaking.

YOU: Dr. Jones, this is Fred Smithers with Beam of Light Financial Services.

DR. JONES: (Interrupting) Excuse me but I am really not interested.

YOU: Sorry to have bothered you. Thank you very much for your time. *Click. Dial tone.*

That was easy, wasn't it?

Since you didn't try to twist Dr. Jones's arm, you at least didn't make an enemy. And he certainly didn't have time to insult you and then grind it in by hanging up on you.

Simple, right?

Right.

THE FIRST PRINCIPLE OF NEW SCHOOL PROSPECTING

Here is a question for you to consider:

What effect do you think you would create on people if, instead of attempting to *keep* everyone you talk to, you try and get rid of them. How will they react?

While you're pondering your answers to these questions, let me tell you something that happened to me.

One benefit to owning my kind of business is I can live where I want. In 1980 I moved from Los Angeles to Sandy, Utah, which is just south of Salt Lake City. (As I write this, I'm in the process of moving back to Southern California. I'm tired of the cold!) Not long after we had arrived and settled in, I got an idea. One thing you'll learn as we progress through this book is that I've had lots of ideas. Some of them are very good, which is why I'm not poor. But some of the ideas have been real turkeys. Probably the reason my company is alive and well is that I kept the good ideas and packed the others off to the great turkey farm in the file cabinet.

At any rate, this particular idea dealt with how to promote our "Public Seminar." Offered by Telephone Marketing, Inc., it was to be a seminar on prospecting to which salespeople in every industry are invited. Some of our programs are geared to the specific needs of a single company or industry, but the public seminar is one virtually anyone can profitably attend.

The idea went like this.

> "I wonder if I can send out a cassette tape of my sales presentation, get various sales managers to play it for their crew, and get some of them so excited that they would show up at a seminar. By doing that, I would at least not have to make that same presentation over and over and over."

It sounded like a good idea to me, so I made up fifteen or twenty copies of a cassette tape, prepared some written material, and then one morning sat down with the Salt Lake *Tribune,* cut out some ads that contained phone numbers, and started calling. (I've always liked calling people who paid money to publish their phone numbers. They tend to answer the phone on or before the third ring.)

One of the first people I called was the local representative of a very well-known sales training course. I figured it would be quite a score to sell them a prospecting course.

My conversation went like this:

ME:	Mr. Jones, this is Bill Good with Telephone Marketing. We specialize in training salespeople to find new business by phone. Tell me, is the telephone at all important to you as a marketing tool?
MR. JONES:	Well, yes. It is.
ME:	Very good. We're having a seminar on February 9 in the Salt Lake Hilton. We have prepared a free cassette tape that will tell you all about it. Would you like to receive a copy of this tape?
MR. JONES:	Well . . . you can send it out if you wanted. We would probably listen to it.
ME:	Well, Mr. Jones, it sounds to me like you have got everything under control there. Since this tape costs us $1.52 to get out the door, if you don't mind I'll just pass at this time. So, thank youverymuch. *Click. Dial tone.*

Now, there probably isn't one of you reading this book that would have just tossed Mr. Jones out of the gold pan as I did. Where there's life, there's hope, right?

So why did I hang up on him?

I hung up on him, because he was *not interested enough!*

I knew I could probably have sold this man a seminar ticket, or perhaps several. But I also knew that to do it, I would have had to first send him the tape, then call him back six times before he would play it for his salespeople. And then I would have had to call him back another three times to find out how many people would be coming to the seminar.

I also knew that I could take the same amount of time I would have spent with him, call rapidly down my list, and find someone who was *very interested* in attending one of my programs.

Yes, I know it is possible to sell people who are initially not interested. But your time is much better spent by letting go those who are not interested and looking for someone who is.

There is no shortage of good prospects!!!

When you find someone who is interested in your product, the relationship goes so much more smoothly that it makes sales a joy, rather than the agony of tooth extraction that many sales trainers have made it.

So the first principle of the New School is:

- **When the prospect says, "I'm not interested,"** *believe* **him or her. Politely hang up. Go find someone who is interested.**

The Thoughts Beneath the Words

I want to introduce you to another concept that plays a key part in this prospecting system: "Actions speak louder than words."

In any verbal communication, there are of course words. And there should be some action. By combining action with words, you enormously increase the power of the communication. So let's take a look at the communication I delivered to Mr. Jones. When I withdrew my offer to send the tape (action) and told him I felt he had everything under control, I delivered another communication as well.

Didn't I tell him that unless he was interested, I wasn't?

Didn't I also tell him I had all the business I could handle?

Suppose I had taken the flicker of interest he showed and just jumped down his throat. What would my actions have said about my product? Wouldn't my actions have said, "This is hard to sell. So just show me a slight glimmer of interest, and we're going to the mat."

What did I say when I told him that I was not going to send him the tape because it cost $1.52? Didn't I tell him, again with my actions, that he was worth less than $1.52? And finally, what did I say when I just hung up, politely of course? Didn't I say, "Listen,

Mr. Jones. There are a lot of people out there who would love to know about this program. So while you're sitting there thinking about it, I'll go find them and you'll miss out."

In short, I delivered a big package of communication to Mr. Jones in just a few words. That's how to put power in your words: Use just a few words and communicate the rest of the thought with an action.

After all, actions do speak louder than words.

THE SECOND PRINCIPLE OF NEW SCHOOL PROSPECTING

The story of Mr. Jones is obviously incomplete as it now stands, and of course, it has a happy ending. Here is what actually happened.

When I'm testing a marketing idea, I do what we call Stage I testing. In Stage I, I normally write a script, get an idea for a prospect list or two (I'll explain more about this in chapters 6 and 7), and then make calls myself to see if it works. I work out any bugs I find, and then when I can make it work, I turn it over to someone else in my organization to do Stage II.

In Stage II, someone whom I have trained makes a lot of phone calls to see if the initial results I got continue to hold. In this case I turned the test over to Jill Olsen, then my assistant and now the general manager of my company, Telephone Marketing, Inc.

We weren't too concerned at this point in our testing with finding out which prospect list was best, so Jill just grabbed the Chamber of Commerce Directory. She started calling and before long she managed to encounter the same Mr. Jones I had spoken with on the first day of my test. The conversation went like this:

JILL: Mr. Jones, this is Jill Olsen with Telephone Marketing.

MR. JONES: (Interrupting) Are you the folks trying to give away that tape?

JILL: (No clue where that remark comes from) Yes, we
                 are.

MR. JONES: I want one.

Needless to say, this time he got a tape. And sent two people
to the course.
So we can conclude:

- **You can call back a list of prospects more than once if you
  don't rough them up the first time.**

How Many Times Can You Recycle a List?

As you'll see in the chapters on list development, a "good list" is
quite obviously an important part of the New School system.
Wouldn't it be wonderful if you didn't have to keep developing
new lists of potential customers but could use some of the old
ones over and over? And what if they got better, not worse?

In other words, if you can call back a list once, maybe you can
call it back several times. How many times can you call back a
list? To answer that question, let's talk for a moment about our
friend, the gold prospector.

Now this old codger went up into Northern California, found
himself a claim on a pretty stream, and began to dig a couple of
ounces of gold right away.

At the end of the first day, you can suppose that he had a tough
question to ask himself: What shall I do tomorrow?

Well, if you were the gold prospector you would of course
answer, "I think I'll stay right here." Two ounces of gold a day is
definitely profitable.

Well, how long will you stay there?

Until all the gold is gone?

Hardly.

Let's say that you have been there for six months. You are only
taking out half an ounce a day. Should you stay or go look for a
better claim?

Well, it depends on the alternatives, doesn't it? You may hear
that upstream they are taking out two ounces a day. Your risk is:

23

Stay for a sure half ounce a day or risk losing that and go for the big strike.

Which do you do?

It depends on how much risk you want to take, doesn't it? Let's say you stay another month. Now your claim is producing only an ounce a week. At this level, it costs you more in supplies than you are making in gold. So naturally you head upstream.

It's the same with a prospect list. Let's say you call a list and get a profitable response. Call the same list again!

The second principle of the New School says:

- **Call a profitable list again in thirty to ninety days.**

How often you call it back depends on the type of product you sell.

In the securities market, where money comes and goes and moves all over the place, you can prospect the same list again every forty-five to sixty days. In residential real estate, try sixty to ninety days. It's about the same for insurance. For automobiles, sixty to ninety days. For expendable supply items, thirty to forty-five days. For commercial real estate, check back every three to four months. For seminars, try every couple of months.

To rephrase the second principle of the New School:

- **Stick with the same claim *as long as it's profitable.***

THE THIRD PRINCIPLE OF NEW SCHOOL PROSPECTING

Believe it or not, you can actually improve the response you get from a prospecting list. And you can improve it by calling it over and over and over again.

The principles you employ to improve a list come basically from mass marketing. We have simply taken them and applied them to the limited market within which most salespeople operate. These four most important principles are:

(1) Repetition.

It has been said that the three main laws that determine the value of a piece of property are Location, Location, and Location. Well the three main laws that determine recognition or familiarity are: Repetition, Repetition, and Repetition.

Major firms use the Principle of Repetition over and over again. On any TV miniseries, you'll see the same ad four to six times per night. Some companies, such as American Express and E. F. Hutton, have had the same basic ad theme running for years. Hutton started their "When E. F. Hutton talks, people listen" campaign in 1969. American Express started the "Do you know my name?" campaign even before that. If large corporations will spend hundreds of millions of dollars repeating the same ad, don't you think it might make sense for a salesperson with a limited market of only fifteen hundred prospects to do the same thing?

Here is a rule of thumb for you:

It takes at least six times for a person to hear your name before he or she will remember it. If you call your prospecting list once, don't be surprised if it doesn't work too well. After you have warmed it up and demonstrated through your actions that you are pleasantly persistent, and that you will be there tomorrow, you will see people begin to recognize you, respond to you, and even call you to request information and even orders.

(2) Make it safe to communicate.

In my opinion, many salespeople deserve the fear the American population puts into them. They have specialized in high-pressure tactics, have pestered and hounded people; and therefore they justly deserve their reputation.

Perhaps those with the worst reputation of all are life insurance salespeople. If any one of you now reading this book is a life insurance salesperson, you know that if you leave a house without a signed contract, you are considered certainly something less than a macho (or macha) salesperson if not a downright wimp or worse, an order taker.

Those of you who have been on the receiving end of a visit from a life insurance agent know just as well that the time came when you had to buy or had to eject the person from your home.

So if you are a life insurance agent, I have good news for you. You too can convince a group of people it's safe to communicate with you. How? Simple. When the prospect says, "I'm not interested," you say "Thankyouverymuch. *Click. Dial Tone.*"

After a time, people will come to believe that it is safe to talk to you. They will understand that you won't jam something down their throats. And at that time, you will find you are no longer making cold calls. You are talking to people you can trust and who can trust you. And after all, who wants to be condemned to making cold calls forever?

(3) Create interest.

Most salespeople have a problem with verbal diarrhea. They feel if they can only cover everything about the product, the prospect will hear something he or she wants and decide to buy.

The opposite is true. You create interest by what you withhold, not by what you disclose.

If in your opening remarks, you offer a benefit and not a description of your product, and if at the first sign of no interest you hang up, you will leave the prospect on the other end of the phone wondering what it is all about.

If you do it again and again and again, you will also have communicated who you are, that you persist to stay in business, and that you have a product in high demand. Otherwise, you would be acting like other salespeople and jamming it down your prospects' throats.

(4) Encourage Word of Mouth.

The easiest way to encourage word of mouth is to select a list on which word of mouth can occur. As a rule, I am truly not even interested in getting started on a list if there is no connection between the prospects on it so that word of mouth can occur. In 1978 I advertised a seminar at the Los Angeles *Times.* Some seventy people showed up, among them a broker from E. F. Hutton and some agents from Farmers Insurance.

After the seminar, I followed up. I sold in-house seminars to

Hutton and Farmers. I got the lists of Hutton branch managers and Farmers district managers. And I started calling and writing. From 1978 to 1980, my trainers and I trained approximately five thousand Farmers agents. In 1980, I did over eighty prospecting seminars for Hutton.

How?

I got lists on which word of mouth could occur and made damned certain it did occur and that it was good! (This same principle can wipe you out if you don't deliver a good product or service.)

Whatever industry you are in, get a list on which word of mouth can occur. In Chapter 6, I'll go over which lists you can get that enable word of mouth to occur.

This brings us to our third principle of the New School:

- **Select a limited market and through the four techniques of list improvement, seek to dominate the market totally.**

To state the principle another way: At any one time, a prospect is located, not created. Over time, through repetition, by making it safe to communicate, by creating interest, and by encouraging word of mouth, good prospects can be created.

THE OLD SCHOOL REVISITED

I trust you see, by now, that there is a certain truth to the Old School that I have retained. If someone says, "I'm not interested," the New School says, "Thankyouverymuchhaveagreatday." But we call him or her back.

In the New School, we only take one no at a time. The Old School will take as many as it can get on one call. But the New School gives you the right to go back, and over time, you will come to own a given market.

So let's move on and talk more of good prospects and where and how to find them.

CHERRY PICKING AND THE FOURTH PRINCIPLE OF NEW SCHOOL PROSPECTING

We'll call our New School method "cherry picking."
This brings us to our fourth principle:

- **On any list, there are some cherries and lots of pits. Pick the cherries, not the pits. But leave the pits on the list.**

So with the idea in mind that we are *prospecting for cherries,* let's define our terms so we know what we're talking about.

Cherries

Cherry: Anyone who is interested, qualified for money, and has the ability to make a decision NOW.

How would we find out if someone is interested?
Simple. We ask.
And how do we find out if they have any money?
Again, we ask.
Will they lie to you?
Yes, some of them will. But we are going to assume people are truth tellers. So even if we know they do have money when they say they don't, we'll believe them.
Let's give a cherry a grade of A. We will use the designation "A" later on to set up an A-B-C call-back file system to help us to keep track of all the prospects we are going to find using this system. (I'll discuss this in detail in Chapter 8.)
For now, let's just assume that A means "active" or "hot" or "cherry" or whatever. An A prospect is any prospect interested and qualified NOW.
When qualifying, we normally first qualify for interest; then, if appropriate, for power to make a decision; and finally, for money. We are going to ignore the question, for now, of what should you do with a qualified prospect once you have identified him or her. Should you send information, set an appointment, or go for an immediate sale? I will come to these questions later in Chapter 4. For now, let's just keep in mind that we are trying to identify a qualified prospect.

Here are some examples of qualifying questions:

In the securities industry:

INTEREST: Mr. Jones, would you like to see some information on this tax-free municipal bond fund?

MONEY: By the way, I am accepting accounts now for $10,000 and above. If you do like the idea, would that amount be a problem to you at this particular time?

In commercial real estate, income residential property:

INTEREST: Have you given any thought to increasing your real estate holdings?

MONEY: If you did find a building you liked, could you handle a down payment of at least $50,000?

In life insurance:

INTEREST: If I could show you how to increase the amount of coverage you now have without spending any more money, would you want to hear about it?

MONEY: If you needed to write a check for a couple of thousand to start the new policy, could you handle that?

For a computer store:

INTEREST: Would you like to see some information on the IBM AT computer?

AUTHORITY: If you did like what you see, would you alone be able to make a decision or would others be involved?

MONEY: Lease payments probably wouldn't run more than $400 a month. If you did like the idea, could you handle that?

29

Green Cherries

Green Cherry: A prospect who indicates interest, but with money and ability to decide at a known later date.

When Telephone Marketing, Inc., trains stockbrokers, we teach that when a prospect says, "I don't have any money," the broker should respond, "Do you expect to have some funds available in the next six months?"

If we find out when money will be available, we have an authentic green cherry, or "greenie," as they are called.

In life insurance, a green cherry would be someone who will give you a birthdate and permission to call back.

In residential real estate, a greenie would be a homeowner who tells you to call back in July because she will have heard by then if she will be transferred. (Call back in June!)

You should definitely keep track of your green cherries, and in most businesses, a substantial portion of new business ultimately will come from the green cherry list. This list you develop, of course, in the process of cold calling.

We give green cherries a grade of B. (A C grade prospect is a someone you have "pitched and missed." It's a downgraded A or downgraded B. We'll cover "C's" also in Chapter 8.)

PITS AND THE FIFTH PRINCIPLE OF NEW SCHOOL PROSPECTING

A pit can be defined as "anyone who is uninterested, unqualified, and/or unable to make a decision." And most salespeople have an intimate knowledge of pits, because they spend the bulk of their prospecting time doing what I call pit polishing.

As an activity pit polishing is singularly unrewarding, consisting as it does of talking to, grinding on, and applying Old School skills to people who are uninterested and unqualified. It is virtually impossible to create interest on a single phone call. Pit polishing is the single biggest destroyer of salespeople that exists.

So here is the fifth principle of New School prospecting. Study it well.

- **Pits are seeds. They sometimes grow into cherry trees. That's why we leave them on the list.**

Hint #1: After talking to a pit, don't write "pit" beside the name. By doing so, you prejudice your list when time comes to call it again. After all, who wants to call a list with "pit" written by most of the names? And initially, most of the names on any list are pits, aren't they?

Hint #2: Don't write down anything by a name unless it's good. It'll save you a lot of time if you only write down the good news.

Hint #3: As a very broad rule, don't take pits off the list. Let me give you an example. In doing some test marketing for our Dental Program recently, I decided to see if this principle held. So I asked my researcher to call back a list of people who less than 2 months earlier had told us they were "happy with their present dentist." Guess what? They acted like they had never received a call from us, and we put lots of cherries in our basket from the list we had called earlier. This is in perfect agreement with the "cherries and pits theory." Now weren't they telling us the truth the first time when they said they were happy? Undoubtedly. *But they came originally from a list that produced a profitable number of cherries.* Like picking cherries from a tree, pick the ripe prospects when they're ripe. Then go back and get some more. After a time, perhaps when you have called the list 6 times or 16 or 66, the list will no longer be profitable. Or it may be unprofitable after the first. Then throw the whole thing out.

Remember, prospecting, as a branch of marketing, deals with groups. Keep everyone but jerks on the list as long as the *list* is profitable. We'll get into how to determine "profitability"—or "how good does a good list have to be?"—in Chapter 6.

Jerks

Regrettably, every list is inhabited by what we have scientifically identified as "jerks." These are the people you call who

31

make you feel bad. Here's how we think such conversations should go:

YOU:	*Ring, ring.*
DR. JONES:	Hello.
YOU:	Is this Dr. Jones?
DR. JONES:	Yes, it is.
YOU:	Dr. Jones, this is Jane Smithers with Beam of Light Financial Services.
DR. JONES:	Are you trying to sell me something? Why you have your nerve calling me at home. Who is your manager, young woman?
YOU:	(banging phone on table three times) Did you hear that sound?
DR. JONES:	(alarmed) Yes. Is there something wrong with the phone?
YOU:	No. That was just opportunity knocking. *Click. Dial tone.*

If you find that a little strong, try this:

DR. JONES:	Are you trying to sell me something? Why you have your nerve calling me at home. Who is your manager, young woman?
YOU:	Oh no. I'm not selling anything. I was just calling to tell you that you are the beneficiary of a very large . . . *Click. Dial tone.*

A word of caution. Please don't misunderstand my thoughts on jerks. They are very few and far between. Yes, I personally have hung up on them from time to time. Maybe four or five times over the past ten years or so. So don't confuse the point here with the drama of its expression.

The point is that under the system I am teaching you in this book, *you are the rejector, not the rejectee.* If in doubt as to whether a particular prospect is a pit or jerk, always remember that good manners is good business.

THE CHERRY PICKER'S ATTITUDE

Since the beginning of time, sales trainers have preached the importance of positive attitude to their sales crews. Frankly, a positive attitude isn't really necessary to be a cherry picker. If anything, you really don't need one at all. What you do need is a "don't care" attitude. Imagine you are sitting at an assembly line. Every minute an item drops out of a chute for you to inspect. It's either a cherry, green cherry, pit, or jerk. You job is to quickly test it and then, depending on what it is, drop it into another chute. Do you care if it's a cherry or not? Of course not. As long as you know what it is.

This don't care attitude is crucial to cherry picking. Here's my explanation of why.

People like doing business with professionals. A professional doesn't get all emotionally involved in whether he or she will succeed or not. The professional just knows that if right actions are taken, anticipated results will follow. No big deal.

Further, professionals have arrived at a point in their careers where they have all the prospects they need. If they had any more, they wouldn't know what to do with them. This *fact of abundance* communicates to the prospect who realizes that it is he or she, the prospect, who must qualify to do business with the professional. And that, according to my theory, is why the don't care attitude is so important.

In other words, the art of assuming the correct attitude is the art of acting like a professional before you may actually be one.

Hint: If you feel you are caring too much, go find a list you really don't care about. Start calling that list. To the very first person who sounds interested, say this:

Mr. Jones. This product probably isn't for you after all. As a matter of fact, if you want it, you'll have to call me. My phone number is 774-3467. Okay?

Actually getting an interested person off the phone is the best therapy I know for someone who "tries" too hard.

THE CHERRY PICKER'S METHOD

The remainder of this book will be a detailed expansion of the method outlined below. I give it to you here in summary form so you can begin practicing its concepts as you go about your work.

1) Develop a prospecting message. (We will be spending a lot of time on the message in subsequent chapters.)

2) Find a good list. (We'll have lots to say about this!)

3) Call the list in a low-key, nonoffensive manner. *Leave the pits on the lists.* (Pits are seeds, remember?) Don't even bother to write down "not in," "not interested," and so on. You'll be calling them back at a different time anyway and then they may well be "in" and "interested."

4) Call the list again in thirty to ninety days. Once again, remove from it people who are cherries and green cherries; you'll be following them up with the methods described in Chapter 5.

5) Continue calling the list back *as long as your response from it compares favorably with the response available from other lists.*

THE CHERRY PICKER'S WAY OF LIFE

Cherry picking is a very pleasant way of life for a salesperson. If someone is not interested, you're not.

If they're unpleasant, don't deal with them. Go look for people you would like to do business with.

And when someone isn't interested, just utter the cry of the cherry picker—thankyouverymuch—and disappear into the electronic haze of the telephone system. Some have even said that "Thankyouverymuch" is the modern equivalent of "Hi-ho, Silver."

Not all your cherries will pan out. Or as the old prospector might say, "Everything that glitters ain't gold. But if there's no glitter, for sure, it ain't gold."

3

What You Say:
To Script or Not

I'm going to start helping you put your telephone-prospecting campaign together with your message. I want you to read the next two chapters very seriously and then grab whatever list you can find. Start calling!

Developing your lists, which I'll cover next, is certainly important. But I don't want you to lose a lot of time working on lists before you start calling, because script and list development can occur simultaneously; and you can fine-tune your scripted message on old prospect lists at the same time you develop new and better lists.

YOUR MESSAGE COUNTS

Suppose you work for Beam of Light Financial Services and you call up a prospect and say:

Jack, this is Fred Smithers down here at Beam of Light. We've got a terrific opportunity here. So I want you to empty out your bank account, bring it down here to the office, and we'll load you up. Okay?

Frankly, with that message, I don't think Jack would set foot out of his house unless it was to come down to your office and punch your lights out.

Quite obviously, the words you say are important. "Wrong words" will stamp out whatever interest you might find. "Right words" will fan a flicker of interest into a flame.

So let's dig in to the subject of the message. Your prospecting message is certainly as important as the list of people you call. If you have an excellent list but deliver a tired, boring message to it, don't expect outstanding results.

Before actually getting into the mechanics of designing the message, let's talk about whether you should have a written script or not. Then we'll take a look at some important strategic questions that will shape your words.

TO SCRIPT OR NOT

Very early in my sales training career, I encountered two phenomena that have always puzzled me. On the one hand, there is no question that a good *written script* gets better results on any list than no script; on the other hand, most salespeople would rather saw off a body part than use a script.

So what exactly is a script?

By "script" I mean a word-for-word treatment of key parts of the prospecting presentation. I do not mean that every single word is scripted. That would be impossible. But I do mean that the *key sections* of the prospecting message should be scripted. (In the next two chapters, you'll see exactly what those key sections are.)

Since most salespeople would prefer to pay parking tickets rather than use a script, and since I believe a written script to be vital, let's take a look at both sides of the issue.

Reasons not to Use a Script

At every seminar I've ever given, I always ask the salespeople attending to write down three reasons why it might *not* be a good idea to use a prepared script. I want you to do that right now. Then I want you to compare your reasons to the reasons below. The ones I'll give, by the way, are the very same ones that occur in *every sales group I have ever worked with*. It is absolutely amazing how consistent salespeople are, from one area of the country to another, from one company to another.

Sales managers take note. The reasons listed below *are the reasons* that your sales crew will give as to why they don't want to use a script. So if you're big on scripts, you better know these well.

1) *It sounds canned.* By this, salespeople mean that the script sounds as if it is being read, not said. Who needs that?

2) *It's "not me."* By this, most salespeople mean that the script isn't written in words they would use. Someone else's words make them feel uncomfortable. And they sound it. So naturally, since it's "not me," they don't want it.

3) *It's not spontaneous.* Surely, an inspired, spontaneous presentation has more life and vitality than an unspontaneous, "canned pitch."

4) *It makes me talk too fast.* When people try a prepared script, they find themselves blabbering on at two hundred words a minute. And once again, the poor written script takes the blame for this.

5) *It's impersonal.* Obviously a presentation that is impersonal won't create a rewarding relationship between salesperson and prospect. Since the script is not written with any one person in mind, it is quite obviously impersonal.

6) *It is inflexible.* This is fairly obvious. A salesperson with decent verbal skills should be able to adapt his or her presentation to each individual rather than lose business due to an inflexible script.

7) *I can't listen.* People feel that when they are reading, they have difficulty listening. And everyone agrees you should listen to the people in your life, prospects included.

8) *I get thrown off.* One of the worst dreads a salesperson has is getting thrown off a script and then groping around at a loss for words. And that definitely can happen.

9) *It's boring.* Frankly, people just get tired of doing the same old thing over and over.

These then are the negatives. In any group of two or more salespeople that talk about scripts, you'll hear these objections to scripts.

I'll bet if you did what I asked you and wrote down your reasons why not to use a script, at least two out of your three reasons were on my list! Most likely all of your reasons were on my list.

Reasons to Use a Script

Now that we've looked at the negative, let's look at the positive. Take just a moment and write down three reasons why it might be a good idea to use a prepared script.

Here are the positive reasons salespeople come up with once they've given it a little thought:

1) *You sound certain.* If you have something to say, you'll sound as though you know what you're talking about. This will handle the "ah"'s and "um"'s and dead spaces that you fear.

2) *You can test.* If you're using a different script on every person you talk to, there is no way you can tell what worked and what didn't work. You've got to hold all variables constant in order to test.

3) *You cover all your important points.* I can't tell you how many salespeople have told me that they have gone through their presentation only to learn that they have forgotten to get the client's bank account number, or some other piece of qualifying data without which they don't have an order.

4) *You can listen better.* When you've got your message worked out, you can concentrate better on what your prospect is saying.

5) *You can make more calls.* If ever there was truth said, this is it. If your message is written down, you're more likely to stick to it. But if you start winging it, you'll thrash around until you have created a bloated message. And your bloat will take much longer to say. Thus a short, neat, phone call becomes a blubbering, lumbering, twenty-minute, pit-polishing phone call.

Let's go back and review the reasons not to use a script, and see if I can't get you to look at scripts in a different light.

1) *It sounds canned.* Certainly, many salespeople, when using a

script, do sound canned. As a matter of fact, when we get into Chapter 9, called "How You Sound," I'll show you exactly the speech elements that cause a canned sound. Once you understand what the canned sound is, and once you have a good script, you can overcome the canned sound through rehearsal.

After all, there is a difference between script preparation and script delivery. Some of us may be good at developing a sales message. Others may be excellent at script delivery; and delivery of a script is really just a question of performance, isn't it? An actor does not create the script. He makes it come alive; and as more than one writer on the subject of sales noted, great salespeople are also great performers.

2) *It's "not me."* This objection to script use is obviously true. To the salespeople who complain, "It's not me," I make the following suggestion. *If you're poor, be someone else.*

There is no reason why anyone should be restricted to one style of sales. Surely you would sell to New York lawyers one way and to North Carolina grain dealers another. If I'm giving my seminar in the Deep South, I'll speak more slowly. I'll let my old North Carolina accent come out. But if I'm in New York City, I will try to tailor my rate of speech, humor, and many of my examples (script, if you please) to a faster-paced audience.

3) *It's not spontaneous.* True. A script is not spontaneous. But, the art in delivering a script is to know it so well that you can deliver it the thousandth time with the same spontaneity as the first time. (Realistically, the first time you gave the speech you probably stumbled through it and didn't sound spontaneous at all. It probably won't even begin to sound good until the hundredth time.)

4) *It makes me talk too fast.* This is a problem with the use of a prepared script. When they get the written word in front of them, many people act like they haven't read aloud since the third grade. (Many haven't.) Instead of reading as they speak, they just fire away at machine gun rate.

The only way I know to overcome this is to take a script and read it aloud about fifty times. Then record it. And then compare a recording of the script with a recording of yourself speaking naturally. Force the script to conform to the way you speak as a human being, not necessarily as a salesperson reading a script.

5) *It's impersonal.* If you just read the script and make no "off the script" comments, it will be impersonal. But that's not necessarily bad. In qualifying prospects for interest and money, there are only so many ways you can do it. There is no problem if you want to get off the script *briefly* to personalize it.

6) *It's inflexible.* A good script *is* inflexible. Any *good* script is designed to find a certain type of prospect. As you try and develop a script that will appeal to everyone, you will wind up appealing to no one.

Here is part of an inflexible script. I call it a gorilla script. A gorilla is someone who is qualified to write a check for $50,000 right away. As you can understand, gorillas might be a bit few and far between, and they don't, frankly, respond the way an ordinary investor does. They are accustomed to being treated differently.

The following is the opening line from a gorilla script I wrote and that has proved to be very effective in prospecting for big money.

> Mr. Jones, this is Bill Good with Acme Securities. You know who we are don't you?
> I'm looking for a very unusual investor this evening. This investor could raise $50,000 for an exceptional opportunity. Does the idea of a $50,000 investment just blow you right out of the saddle? (This script was written in Texas so you can understand the use of the word "saddle.")

Another gorilla script that I wrote in Richmond, Virginia, contained the phrase, "Does the idea of $100,000 blow you out of the water?"

As you can see, this particular script is *very inflexible.* It only looks for one particular type of investor, the one who can cut a check for $50,000. Those with $5,000 or $10,000 need not apply.

The idea behind the inflexibility of a good script is that you, as a prospector, should set in mind the kind of prospect you want and then go after that type of person. If someone does not meet your requirements, go find someone who does. Remember, we're not trying to sell everybody. Just those who are interested, qualified, and with whom *you want to do business.* A good script is inflexible and will find you the kind of prospect you're looking for.

7) *I can't listen.* You really can't, until you've rehearsed the script. But if you'll spend somewhere between ten minutes and an hour reading your script aloud, over and over, you'll find that you can actually listen better.

8) *I get thrown off.* There is no question whatsoever that you can be thrown off. I'll never forget a young man in Des Moines, Iowa, who was reading a particular paragraph of a script, got asked a question, forgot his place, and then began to read the same paragraph again.

All the color suddenly drained from his face, and I heard him stutter, "I'm . . . . not . . . . doing a very good job. Suppose I call you back later, Okay? Thankyouverymuch. *Click. Dial tone.*" Remember, the system you're learning in this book does contain an ejection seat. If you get in trouble, press the button!

9) *It's boring.* We did a scientific study at Harvard not long ago and discovered, to everyone's surprise, that salespeople like making money. We then asked 4,085 salespeople if they had a script that was making money for them, would they be bored? Three replied that yes, they would be bored. On further investigation, it was found that two of these were independently wealthy anyway, and one was a part-time welfare worker who believed that money was the root of all evil. But the other 4,082 salespeople interviewed replied they most certainly would not be bored.

So what's boring about using a script?

Getting no results is boring, very boring. *So when you find yourself getting bored, chances are you're doing something wrong and are not getting results!*

REASONS TO USE A SCRIPT

The reasons sales people give *to use a script* are all true. I would like to offer two more of my own.

1) Top sales people use scripts.

Now, you may not find that they have their scripts written down. But they are there. They are in their heads. And if you ever have an opportunity to listen to a top salesperson give a presentation twice, you will see not just similarities, but identical passages. He or she has worked these words out over the years and wouldn't change them for anything.

I was fortunate on two occasions to be able to sit through a seminar given by one of the million-dollar producers at E. F. Hutton. This man is a specialist in managed commodities accounts, and when I heard his one-hour seminar the first time, I learned a lot, not only about managed commodities but about seminar structure and design. It was brilliant.

Then I heard it again. The thing that struck me the second time I heard it was that the speech was virtually identical to the first time I heard it.

Once over lunch with him at a conference in Reno, Nevada, I asked him, "John, don't you get tired of giving that same old seminar over and over again?" He looked at me as if I had just asked one of the world's most stupid questions. His answer, with a shrug: "If it ain't broke, don't fix it."

He had his script. It was a seminar script. The idea that he would change it was incomprehensible. He was using it to put a lot of money in his pocket year after year. I've listened to other greats. And I find that they do the same thing over and over again. It's the new kid on the block who feels compelled to be unique and creative each and every presentation. The old kid on the block long since tried that out and found that some sets of words work better than others. And since he wanted to go to the bank instead of the poorhouse, he'd stick with the one that worked. And even if it causes brain damage to give the same presentation over and over again, he'll laugh all the way to the bank.

2) Words create effects.

This may seem self-evident but it is nevertheless true. You were, I hope, taught by your parents that honey catches more flies than vinegar. To put it another way, it's not just what you say, it's *exactly* what you say that counts.

Consider these very slight changes in well-known advertising slogans.

MacDonalds: We do it all to you.

E. F. Hutton: When E. F. Hutton talks, some people listen.

AT&T: Reach out and grab someone.

As you can see, changing even a single word can make a material change in meaning and therefore effect. When you get a good script, one that delivers predictable and profitable results, if you change it, it's a sign of advanced brain damage. Don't do it.

YOU WILL USE A SCRIPT

As a final argument for using a written, word-for-word script, try this. If you're going to be making high volume phone calls, there is no way after the fiftieth call that you will have failed to develop a script. It is impossible to make fifty rapid *and unique* phone calls. It won't happen. What will happen is that by the fiftieth call, you will have a script. It will be one that you have settled into, and more likely than not, will contain such gems as, "Mr. Jones, I was wondering if maybe . . ."

So you will use a script. The only question is: Will you write it down in advance or just fall into it?

Now that we have settled the argument as to whether you'll have a script or not, we need to discuss some basic strategy of the script. Your answers to the questions I am going to go over below will shape your script. So please give very careful thought to these questions, my comments, and your own answers.

ON THE FIRST CALL, SHOULD YOU TALK ABOUT SERVICE, CONCEPT, OR PRODUCT?

Let's first define some terms:

Service: Something you can do for someone.

Concept: A group of related products. Blue chip stocks, apartment buildings, photocopiers: All of these are *concepts.*

Product: Something you can write an order for. You can buy or sell a thousand shares of IBM. You can buy or sell the apartment building at 405 Dokes Street. You can rent or lease a Xerox photocopier. These are all products.

In almost any industry, there is some choice about what to talk about on the first call. You can talk about service, concept, or product.

Take fire extinguishers.

You *could* talk about a service. The service you could offer would be a free home safety examination that would, most likely, end in a finding that the prospect needs more fire extinguishers.

Or, you *could* talk about the broad *concept* of fire extinguishers and their importance to the home and family safety.

Finally, you *could* talk about a specific fire extinguisher that you would like to sell or at least get an appointment to show.

So where do you start? Service? Concept? Product?

My answer is: PRODUCT. A specific product. If you are selling fire extinguishers, talk about the fire extinguisher that sells best in the type of market you're calling, and do that *even if you have an entire catalog full of fire extinguishers.*

Here's why.

With every company I've worked, in every market, in every part of the country, I have been able to get better results talking about PRODUCT. And that's true even for such service-oriented industries as life insurance. I have found that the more specific you make your phone call, the more likely you are to discover interest and qualification. And the more likely you are to get people to make up their minds one way or the other.

Let's take the securities industry, where I have done my most extensive research on this question. When I began doing my research in the securities industry in the fall of 1978, the conventional wisdom stated that a stockbroker should offer a service. A typical first call went like this:

Mr. Jones, this is Brad Bradshaw. I'm over here at Wiggins and Wanstrop. If you don't mind, I'd like to take a few minutes of your time, run a few questions by you, and see if there isn't something we can do for you.

As I watched brokers make this kind of call hour after hour, it became apparent that it was one tough row to hoe. Worse, after forty-five minutes or an hour or so, the brokers themselves had become extremely discouraged; and that discouragement had begun to color their voices and so was bringing about the negative result they sought to avoid.

But in spite of what seemed to me to be highly unsatisfactory results and morale, "everyone" seemed to agree that "service" was the way to go. "Need satisfaction" selling was, after all, the order of the day.

As I studied this approach, I began to realize that the era in which the service approach came of age was quite different from the era of the late 1970's. The service approach was born in an era when brokers were only hired if they had family or social connections. A service approach is appropriate where *connections already exist.* But what about the broker whose father was a garbage truck driver? His connections are certainly not going to make him rich. Will the service approach work for him? Or will it be a bust, as it seemed to me to be?

So I began a series of tests that went on for quite some time. I would split a group of brokers in half. The first group would use the usual service approach. The second group would call on a product. Or the first half would call on a concept and the second half on a service. You get the idea.

Sometimes, my results on calling with a product absolutely bombed, and service was better. My breakthrough came one night when I was testing a particular product approach. Nothing was happening. I was calling the Palos Verdes Peninsula in Southern California (lots of money), and I got tired of the script I was using. So I pulled another one out of my file and tried it. Results *instantly* improved. No one in Palos Verdes wanted to hear about an annuity, which is what I was experimenting with on my first script. Within twenty minutes, however, I found four tax shelter prospects. Looking back, I had found a *specific product that a list was interested enough in to make my calls extremely profitable. What else did I need? Nothing. End of test.*

Conclusion: You have to marry product and list to make it work!

If you absolutely cannot find a product that is profitable to talk about on the first call, then fall back and try a conceptual approach. And finally, as a last resort, before using your list to line the bottom of your birdcage, try service.

If what you really want to do is talk service, FIRST TALK PRODUCT. Why? Because it works. Just try it.

THE PRODUCT APPROACH

Here's what I do.

1) Pick a product.

2) Write a script stressing the one or two best benefits of that product. Ask for interest. Then money. (Don't worry. In the next two chapters, we'll cover the mechanics of script writing.)

3) Test the script with a given list. If in fairly short order, you're not getting good results (we'll define "good results" later), work on the wording of your script. Make more calls. Then switch products. If you're still not getting three an hour, refine your script. If you still can't get your three, and if you've tested the other variables as discussed in Chapter 11, you might try a conceptual approach, or finally a service approach. I have long since dispensed with the conceptual and service approaches. If I can't find a product of sufficient interest to a list of people that I can get three cherries an hour, I'll keep switching products or lists. I've done it too many times to suspect otherwise. And I'll find the combination in two days at the most.

IF YOU ONLY SELL A SERVICE

If your "product" is a service, you're in deep trouble on this approach, right?

No. Just sell it like a product.

Suppose you sell a consulting service. Just package it so that it

46

has a fixed price and accomplishes a verifiable result. For $1200 (or whatever), tell your customer "what's wrong and what it will take to fix it." Or if you sell "financial planning," sell the plan, not the process. If you sell janitorial services, sell clean buildings. If you sell carpet cleaning, sell "clean carpets." If you sell architecture, sell "planned buildings."

Or take seminars, which I sell. A seminar is really a packaged consulting service offering a solution that applies to similar businesses. So while I deliver a service, I package and sell it like a product.

So if you sell service, figure out what the end result of it is, assign a fixed price to at least the first sale, and sell it like a product. I used to wonder why there was so little good material in sales literature on selling services as opposed to product. The reason, of course, is that those who have mastered "service sales" sell a service like it's a product. There is no separate subject of "selling intangibles."

WHAT SHOULD BE THE OBJECTIVE OF THE FIRST CALL?

In many industries, it has long since been chiseled in stone that the objective of the first call should be: Get the appointment.

In insurance, this is certainly an article of faith no longer even open to question. (Some agents have even been taught to get in the door without telling the prospect what they are coming there to talk about. I call this "the mystery lead approach." We'll cover it in detail in Chapter 5.) In real estate, people are taught the absolute importance of getting in the door, and various techniques have been developed over the years to accomplish this objective.

Well, I think it's time to reevaluate what should be the objective of the first phone call. So as our first principle, let's set down a hard-and-fast rule and chisel it in stone.

- **In determining the objective of the first call, there are no hard-and-fast rules chiseled in stone.**

And now a second one:

47

- **The objective you set for your first call will be determined by the resistance level of your list.**

By "objective" I mean the end result you seek for a given contact by phone. For example, an objective *might be* an appointment. I'll expand on this in a moment, but first I want to show you how the objective you select will *shape your script.* Let me give you an example of some test marketing we did for a computer store.

The Computer Store

One market I have always been interested in for my seminars is microcomputers. Aside from being quite a microcomputer enthusiast myself and having built a substantial portion of my business on two early models, I believe that computer stores, like many other retail businesses, can certainly supplement their mass marketing with a direct telephone campaign.

Like sales personnel at car dealers, appliance dealers, and many other "big ticket" retailers, most salespeople in computer stores sit and wait for something to happen. Much of that sitting-and-waiting time could actually be spent sitting at a desk, calling people, and getting them into the store. Besides, it's a lot cheaper to get someone in the door by phone than it is through radio, TV, or print advertising.

At any rate, the whole thing started with the salesman who had sold me my computers. In the course of getting to know each other before he became a manager, he found out what I did and one day asked for some help in generating some business. I sold him a set of cassette tapes, told him to listen to them, and said if he needed any additional help I'd give him a hand.

Well, he went to work and built his own sales up from $3,000 per month to well over $60,000 per month, which he attributed simply to getting on the phone and calling people and inviting them into the store for seminars. Subsequently, he was promoted to manager of one of the major computer stores.

As a result of his work, I knew we could call people up and get them into the store for a seminar. But what about those times when we didn't have a seminar scheduled. Then what? We decided to do some tests. And here is where I learned a thing or two about the objective of the phone call.

There was a new microcomputer model out, quite impressive. So I sent one of my staff down to the store with a script I had written. The first script was simply a call to qualify for interest and money and then invite someone in for an appointment to see the computer.

After making several hundred phone calls, I knew we had a flapping turkey on our hands. Initially, the people we called seemed interested, but they resisted the idea of coming into the store. And it really wasn't practical to take the equipment to the prospect. The salespeople in the store were not excited at all about lugging their gear all over town.

So I rewrote the script and *reduced the commitment level required by the prospect.* In other words, I cut back the objective of the phone call.

Instead of asking people if they would come into the store, we simply called and inquired if they were interested in seeing some information on the new computer. If yes, we sent it to them. And then we called them back a second time.

Old School Resistance Handling

Had I been an Old Schooler, I would certainly have handled the problem differently. I would have first analyzed all the objections people gave for not wanting to come into the store. I would have come up with a list of excuses, such as "too busy," "too far away," and so forth.

Then I would have trained the salespeople to respond instantly to these objections by "power closing" the prospect. The Old School teaches, after all, that "an objection is an opportunity to close." This probably would have led to the normal exhaustion-hate relationship that usually exists between Old Schoolers and prospects.

Handling Resistance in New School Style

If anything, the New School could be called the low IQ approach because its answers are so simple. Most salespeople are high IQ and so miss the simplicity of prospecting and sales.

If I'm running into resistance, instead of figuring out compli-
cated systems to get people to do what I want them to do, I just
figure out something they will do *today*. If this leads where I want
to go, I'll settle for it and save my effort and stress for something
else.

So if the prospects don't want to come see me, I'll try and go
see them. If that's a problem, I'll see if they are interested enough
to let me send them some information. And that's about as low
as I'll go.

It really is that simple.

After I redrafted my new model script, I sent my researcher
back over to the computer store to make another hundred or so
phone calls. Within a half hour she called excitedly and said, "It's
working."

Here's another point to chisel in stone.

> • **When a campaign is failing, it's absolutely miserable to work
> with. But when you have made the right change, you know
> it very quickly. It doesn't take forever.**

I can't tell you how many times, whether in real estate, insurance,
the securities industry, the computer industry, or whatever, I have
tinkered with a campaign and then all of a sudden it's right! There
is a world of difference between a campaign that is not working
and one that is. When you've got it right, it's a joy to deal with.

SO WHAT SHOULD BE THE OBJECTIVE OF THE FIRST CALL?

The place to start when developing a new campaign or revising
a failing campaign is with the objective of the first call. There are
at least eleven possible objectives to set for a single phone call:

1) Sell something

2) Get a commitment as to when the person will decide when to buy

3) Open the account

4) Set an appointment—your office

 5) Set an appointment—their office

 6) Tentative appointment

 7) Qualify for interest and money

 8) Qualify for interest only

 9) Invite to seminar

10) Add to mailing list

11) Simply inform

The Scale of Commitment

As you look over the list of possible objectives above, you may notice that I have arranged them in order of decreasing commitment required by the prospect.

This concept of a scale of commitment, which goes from very little commitment on the part of the prospect to quite a bit at the top level, is a critical concept for you to understand if you are to use the objective correctly in developing your script.

Here is how to work with the objective.

1) Pick an objective and draft a script to achieve it.

2) Test it out.

3) Where you encounter stiff resistance toward the close of your phone call, cut back on the commitment level required and retest. If your initial script was designed to get someone to come to your store or office, and that fails, try getting them to agree to accept information and then qualify for money. If you get resistance to that, invite them to a free seminar. If there is tremendous resistance there, call and ask if they would like to be added to the mailing list. If you get resistance to that, try just informing them of something of interest. And if that doesn't work, get another list and start over.

Don't you see that that's exactly what happened in our series of computer tests? In the first test, we were not getting any commitments although we were talking to plenty of people. And my researcher reported that they were actually resisting our invitation to visit the store. So instead of using the Old School "overcome objections" style of selling, we just asked for less. We went from no results per hour to an average of five people per hour who wanted to see the information and could handle a lease payment in excess of $300 per month.

In calling those back the following week, approximately half agreed to come into the store, and of the appointments scheduled, a substantial percentage held.

Subsequently, I trained six people in that store, and in a one-hour blitz, we found lots of prospects. Over the next six weeks, those prospects generated $19,000 in business. That's $3000 of new business generated *per salesperson hour on the phone.* Not bad.

So don't be a whole hog salesperson. If you want to sell something, you may be able to do it on the first call, but you may not. The correct way to evaluate results is in terms of how much time it takes you to achieve what you want. Forget whether that time may be spent today or over a period of weeks.

Far better to make twenty one-minute phone calls than one twenty-minute phone call that ends in failure.

Correct use of the objective is a powerful tool. Use it and profit.

GO FOR INTEREST AND MONEY

Because of extensive testing, I am going to first teach you a multi-call approach. In Chapter 4, you'll learn how to qualify for interest and money on the first call. In Chapter 5, you'll learn how to set the appointment on a second call. We'll also discuss how to set appointments on the first call, but I rarely even bother writing scripts to sell or even set appointments on first call. Most markets are too resistive. So I take the easy way and just see if there is some interest and money there. If yes, well, I've found a cherry.

You can compare what I am doing to direct mail. A direct mailer sends out "bulk mail." I send out "bulk phone calls." The direct mailer receives responses, also called "leads." I find cherries, also called leads.

A salesperson who receives the bulk mailer's leads calls them and sets appointments. The appointment call is the *first call,* but it is not the first contact. The letter that generated the response card was the first contact.

A salesperson who receives the leads from a "direct phoner," (or who does the direct phoning himself or herself) receives some cherries. A second call is made to set the appointment.

The next chapter will show you how to write a script to find your cherries.

4

Script Writing—Part I: Finding Your Cherries with the First of Two Calls

Although I have never done it, I am sure that writing radio commercials requires some of the same discipline that writing telephone scripts imposes.

Both radio commercial and telephone scripts must be short. Each deals with voice only. A wrong word can blow either out of the water. Also, as with telephone script writing, I imagine it would be difficult to become a good radio commercial writer. And as a matter of fact, if I had to learn to do it, I would get hold of a collection of the best radio commercials ever written, and I would rewrite each several hundred times, adapting it to suit my product or service. By so doing, I would learn the structure and form of a good commercial. I know I would never learn it by just reading one. Nor will you learn how to write good telephone scripts if you just read the examples in this chapter. Frankly, the best way to learn how to write them is to first rewrite them. Take a script that doesn't have anything to do with you. Rewrite it until it does. That's how to learn, and that's how I'm going to teach you.

BEFORE YOU START: WHAT YOU NEED TO KNOW

Quite obviously, before you rush in to begin script writing, you need to bring certain information about your product or service to the forefront of your mind. So let's talk for just a moment about what people actually buy.

The idea that people buy benefits, not features, is certainly not original with me. It's just what they buy. Automobile companies long since figured out that people don't buy cars or even transportation. They buy sex appeal and image. And you won't find any single part of the car that houses these.

So what's a feature? And what's a benefit?

FEATURE: What something is.

BENEFIT: What that feature does for the prospect.

Here are some examples:

ITEM: Coffee cup.

FEATURE: Made of bone china.

BENEFIT: Not only lovely to look at and hold but something you would want your grandchildren to have.

ITEM: Ball-point pen.

FEATURE: Has blue ink.

BENEFIT: Makes it easy to read.

So here is what you need to do:

1) Write down ten features of your product or service.

2) Write down a *benefit of each.*

3) Now write down what would qualify a person to buy your product. You will need that information when the time comes to write your script.

This is certainly not a difficult exercise. But it is only so important that your script will probably flop if you don't do it.

RULES FOR REWRITING SCRIPTS

There are a few simple rules for rewriting proven scripts.

1) Pick a script that accomplishes what you want to accomplish.

2) Rewrite one part of a script at a time, and keep rewriting until it reads smoothly when you read it aloud. Then go to the next part.

Here's an example of what I mean by rewriting:

55

ORIGINAL (for securities industry): M/M _____, I have some important information for investors on what's called a tax-free municipal bond fund. Have you ever heard of one of these before?

REWRITTEN FOR COMPUTER SALES: M/M _____, I have some important information for you on our Armadillo computer. Have you seen the ads we've been running on TV?

In other words, by rewrite I mean take one of the scripts I will go over with you and make it fit your product and your market.

3) No sentence should contain more than fourteen words. Long sentences are fine for school themes, especially when you don't have much to say and need to pad. But they are not good for sales, which is spoken, not written. In spoken English, your listener can't go back to the beginning of one of these long, tortured sentences to see what you started out to say.

Very often, in rewriting a script, you will notice you have produced one of these fifty-five-word monster sentences. Rewrite the sentence into several shorter ones.

4) No technical words. It is never safe to assume that a prospect is as well educated as the salesperson.

Some prospects even think a debenture (which is a kind of bond) is what you put in your glass of water on your bedside table at night. Points are what you get in a game of bridge. And a listing is what you get in the phone book.

So edit out complex and technical words.

5) Don't talk more than fifteen seconds without asking a question. If a prospect does not get involved in the conversation, you've lost. Questions are the salesperson's tool for creating involvement. Also, they help you establish control. In the conversation below, you tell me who is in control.

DAUGHTER: Daddy, why does it rain?

FATHER: Well, uh . . . tiny little drops of water get together and become big drops. They fall down.

DAUGHTER: Why do they fall down instead of up?

FATHER: Uh . . . gravity. It's gravity that calls them down to the earth, sort of like you call your dog.

DAUGHTER: But why?

FATHER: I guess because that's what it wants to do.

DAUGHTER: How far is it to the moon?

FATHER: Uh . . . it's . . . uh . . .

Another reason for asking lots of questions is: How else will you know if your prospect is still awake?

Finally, asking questions enables you to control what the prospect thinks about. If you simply stop talking, the prospect's attention can just wander off. But the question directs his or her attention to the area you want the prospect to think about.

6) When you write don't edit; when you edit don't write. This particular rule was taught to me by a very old and very dear friend of mine when I lived in New York in the late 1960's. I had decided that I wanted to become a professional writer, but I was enormously inhibited by a tortured, academic writing style and by writer's block. She explained to me that the major cause of writer's block is trying to write and edit at the same time. To prevent that, she made me write whatever came to mind *and only then* to edit.

Writing is creative. Editing is corrective. To correct what you are creating while it is being created will stop the creation as surely as a blow to the head.

With these rules of script *rewriting* in mind, let's take a look at different script styles. As you study the styles and the different examples of them, be on the lookout for one that you like. I would recommend, however, that you try one of each.

THE FIRST CALL: QUALIFICATION SCRIPT

A qualification script is designed to find cherries. It is not designed to set an appointment or to sell. We will reserve that for the second call. In your first call, you offer your prospects some written information to see if they are interested, and then, if they are, you ask two or three key qualification questions. One question is ALWAYS about M O N E Y. The qualification script has nine parts. Below, I will define each part and give an example of it. Then I will give you several different complete scripts. And finally, I will give you a Script Development Form. You can use this as a guide to rewriting your own script.

Here are the parts of a qualification script:

1) The Introduction

The introduction establishes communication with the prospect and answers the two questions that anyone wants to know: who you are and what company you are with. You then ask a question that's got a simple yes or no answer, and one that provides the prospect an opportunity to let you know he or she's not a cherry. (Remember, a major goal on first calls is *disqualification*. We're not trying to hang onto everyone we talk to.)

EXAMPLE OF INTRODUCTION

May I speak with M/M _____, please? (RESPONSE) M/M _____, this is _____ with (COMPANY). You know who we are, don't you?

IF NO: We're the ones that specialize in helping you keep more of your hard-earned money.

Where your prospect may not be familiar with your firm, an alternate acceptable question is:

May I speak with M/M _____, please? (RESPONSE) M/M _____, this is _____ with (COMPANY). Does the name (COMPANY) ring a bell?

IF NO: We're the ones that specialize in helping you keep more of your hard-earned money.

In a highly resistant market, you can use the phrase:

Can you hear me okay on this phone?

The "hear me okay" question ALWAYS gets a yes or a no. It's actually an "attention diversion" question and gets the prospect's attention off of whatever he or she may be resisting at the moment.

2) The Offer

Once you have the prospect's attention, make an offer. In a qualification script, the best offer seems to be some written information. If it takes you longer than one or two sentences to make your offer, you need to break up the long-windedness with a question. You will also need to use a question when you have good reason to suspect your prospect may not be familiar with your offer or product.

Here are some examples of "offers" from different industries. As you read these, keep in mind they represent only offers made in the "qualification style."

TAX-FREE BOND FUND—SECURITIES INDUSTRY:

M/M _____, I have some important information for you on what's called a tax-free municipal bond fund. Have you ever heard of one of these before?

COMMERCIAL REAL ESTATE:

I have some information available on an eight-unit apartment building we have for sale.

VARIABLE (OR UNIVERSAL) LIFE INSURANCE:

I have some important information on how to get a higher rate of return on your money than a CD.

Comment: Variable life or universal life can be sold as life insurance. Or, it can be sold as an investment with life insurance. It's this latter approach I have found most instructive.

CERTIFICATE OF DEPOSIT (CD)—BANKING

M/M _____, I have some very important information for you on a guaranteed investment.

Assignment: Write an offer for your product or service. Use one of the examples given as your model.

3) The Opening Benefit

The opening benefit statement comes right after the offer and tells the prospect what benefit he or she will get by accepting the offer.

In the examples below, I have reprinted the offers I used above. The opening benefit statements follow and are printed in **bold-face.**

TAX-FREE BOND FUND—SECURITIES INDUSTRY:

M/M _____, I have some important information for investors on what's called a tax-free municipal bond fund. Have you ever heard of one of these before?

(Yes or No) **Okay. Basically (as you know), it's a portfolio of top quality, tax-free municipal bonds that have been selected for both income and safety.**

Comment: The yes-or-no phrase indicates that we really don't care whether the person has or has not heard about tax-free municipal bond funds. We're going to tell 'em anyway. I found out that a lot of people thought they knew what such things were and didn't. The phrase "as you know" is inserted if the prospect claimed he or she knew.

COMMERCIAL REAL ESTATE:

I have some information available on an eight-unit apartment building we have for sale. **I'm calling to find out if you have given any thought at all to increasing your real estate holdings and possibly even becoming rich?**

Comment: Here the offer is imbedded in a question. Some commercial real estate agents have trouble asking this question. They think it sounds hokey. Maybe. But it works. Many people who have invested in commercial real estate did so with one motive: to get rich. Most haven't made it yet. You'll get their attention with this question. (Of course, some of them will say, "No." They're already rich.)

VARIABLE LIFE INSURANCE:

I have some important information on how to get a higher rate of return on your money than a CD. **The interest compounds. Uncle Sam doesn't touch it at tax time. And if something should happen to you, your family would get a whole bunch of money.**

CERTIFICATE OF DEPOSIT (CD)—BANKING

M/M _____, I have some very important information for you on a guaranteed investment. **It's a bank CD and it's paying _____ percent.**

Assignment: Write lots of possible opening benefit statements for your product or service.

4) The Interest Question

Following your offer and opening benefit statement, you want to find out: Is your prospect interested? To discover interest, ask a question. But you need to make certain your question matches up with your offer and is not, at this stage, a thinly disguised closing question.

Here's how to do it wrong:

M/M _____, I have some important information for investors on what's called a tax-free municipal bond fund. Have you ever heard of one of these before?

(Yes or No) Basically, as you know, it's a portfolio of top quality, tax-free municipal bonds. These have been selected for both income and safety. **Are you interested?**

Comment: The question "Are you interested?" is too strong at this point in the conversation. Many people will feel that a "Yes" to that question commits them to buy, and so they'll say "No, I'm not." A better question would be: "Would you like to take a look at a report on this fund?" This lets the prospect express interest without making too much of a commitment so early in the relationship.

So keep in mind that the interest question is designed to see if the prospect is interested in your offer, not, at this point, in getting together with you or in buying your product. If you offered information, your question should ask if they **are interested in that!** Here are two examples.

- Would you like to take a look at a report on this fund?
- Could I send you some information on it?

While I have used the first question for a long time, my current favorite is number two. It seems to be a bit easier for people to answer.

Assignment: Pick the interest question you want to use. Or rewrite one of your own.

5) Not Interested at All

This is a line that is standard in every script. When you hear a firm "I'm not interested," your response is always Thank youverymuch.

6) Fallback

If you don't study very carefully what I am about to say, you will think I just undercut what I said in Number 5 above. Let's define the fallback as "that portion of the script you use when the prospect is not interested in your offer but his or her behavior indicates he may be interested in something." If you misunderstand what I'm saying here, YOU WILL WIND UP WASTING A LOT OF TIME WITH PITS. IF THE PROSPECT SAYS FIRMLY, "I'M NOT INTERESTED," BELIEVE! GO ON TO THE NEXT CALL.

Here's a sample conversation:

YOU: Could I send you some information on our tax-free municipal bond fund?

PROSPECT: I don't think a bond fund is the right thing for me at this time.

YOU: Okay. What kind of investments have you been making lately?

PROSPECT: Mostly mutual funds.

YOU: Great! If I come up with a good mutual fund idea, you wouldn't mind if I called you back and mentioned it to you, would you?

PROSPECT: No. That would be fine.

YOU: Okay. By the way, I normally accept accounts of $10,000 and above. If you do like the idea, would that amount normally be a problem to you?

PROSPECT: No, I could handle that if it were something I liked.

YOU: Great! Now in case I can't catch up with you during the day, how can I reach you during the evening?

PROSPECT: My number is 555-4444.

YOU: Great! If I come up with something, I'll give you a call, okay?

PROSPECT: Okay.

YOU: Great! You have a nice day and thank you for your time. *Click. Dial tone.*

Comment: First, I didn't offer to send the prospect out some information right away. Why not? Answer: I didn't want to appear to be one of those salespeople who have something for everybody. I called him on a bond fund idea, and quite frankly, I really don't want to appear too interested in another area. I am! But I don't wish to appear to be.

Second, use a fallback when your primary offer fails. But do so ONLY when the prospect indicates in manner or behavior that some interest or openness exists.

Third, let's consider, for a moment, what kind of prospect we have identified with our fallback and where to file him. Let's call him an A- and phone him in a week or ten days. At that time, we'll qualify for money if we haven't done so already, and, if he's qualified, then go straight for the appointment.

Fourth, you will usually fall back when your prospect is not interested in your offer. If you have qualified for money and the prospect is broke, don't fall back. Find out when the prospect will have some money.

Assignment: Rewrite several possible fallbacks for your product or service.

7) Qualification

Once you have established interest, it's time to see if your prospect has the *capability* to carry through. In this section, you'll be asking some very direct questions. Don't worry about offending people with directness, since the only people you'll offend are most likely the poor and non-decision makers. Here we separate the fisherpersons from the bait cutters.

As you will see, the questions you'll be asking are normally "closed end." A closed end question is any question that can be answered with a yes or a no. They are point blank and in addition to weeding out the bait cutters, you'll get rid of the bush beaters as well. Remember, one definition of a pit is someone who cannot make up his or her mind. We want to find those early, since the major killer of salespeople is not the ones who say no, but the people who say maybe.

Here is how you might qualify someone who is interested in a report on a municipal bond fund.

> If I send this information out today, you should receive it by (DAY).
> Will you have time to look it over by (DAY)? (RESPONSE) If you do
> like the idea, would an investment of ($_____) be a problem to you
> at this particular time?

Assignment: Carefully craft a "qualifies" portion of your script. Then rewrite it several times.

8) Qualifies

If your prospect does qualify, wrap up the conversation and get off the phone. Here is a continuation of the bond fund script. The phrase in parentheses is optional. Use it if you want to make certain the money is there now.

> (Are these funds available now?) Just one other question and I'll let
> you go. In case I can't get in touch with you during the (DAY/EVEN-
> ING), how can I reach you during the (DAY/EVENING)? I have your
> address down as _____. Is that correct? Great! Haveagoodday and
> thankyouverymuch.

Assignment: Decide what you will say *if your prospect QUALI-FIES*. Write this down. Now rewrite it until it feels good.

9) Does Not Qualify

If the prospect is interested but not qualified now, all we want to know is: When will he or she have the money? If the person is not a cherry now, when will he or she likely be one?

Continuing with the bond fund script, here is how you would look for a green cherry.

> Is this just a temporary condition or do you have any monies coming due in the next six months? (RESPONSE) Very good. Suppose I get back to you in (MONTH), okay?

Assignment: Rewrite what you'll say if your prospect is interested but DOES NOT QUALIFY.

Properly done, the entire qualification script should take not more than one minute from start to finish. Most calls will be much shorter since the vast majority of people do disqualify and will do so earlier rather than later in the presentation.

DETERMINING AUTHORITY TO BUY

In selling products or services directly to a consumer, you really don't have much problem in identifying your decision maker. There are a few problems, and we'll come to those. It's much harder, however, to determine "authority to buy" when dealing with a corporation. So let's spend a few minutes on that first.

Finding Out Who Buys at a Corporation

Surely, one of the biggest time wasters is talking with someone who cannot spend money. Regrettably, many corporations are populated by people who can say no but not yes. Ideally, you want to spend your time with the decision maker, but unfortunately, a lot of decision makers got to be that way by learning how to delegate parts of their job. They'll use subordinates, for example, to screen salespeople and their proposals, while reserving to themselves the right to say yes. Unfortunately, if you try to sneak past the people who can say no but not yes, they'll sabotage you. So go through channels, but just find out quickly what the channel is and if the person who can say no can also lead you to the yes sayer.

Suppose you are selling photocopiers. First try and find out who buys them by asking the receptionist. Then verify that when you get to the decision maker's secretary. Then nail it down again with the decision maker. Note below the use of the word "alone."

TO RECEPTION:	Good morning. This is Fred Smithers. I need to speak with the person there who buys your office equipment, computers, copiers, big stuff like that. Could you tell me his or her name, please?
TO SECRETARY:	Good morning. This is Fred Smithers with Acme Office Equipment. I understand M/M _____ is the person there at (COMPANY) that buys your bigger office equipment, is that correct? (RESPONSE) Could you connect me please?
TO DECISION MAKER:	Good morning. This is Fred Smithers with Acme Office Equipment. I understand you're the one there at (COMPANY) who **alone** buys your copiers, computers, bigger office equipment. Is that correct?

Finding Out Who Buys at Home

If I'm ever going to be shot for being a male chauvinist, it will be for what I am about to recommend to you. If it sounds male chauvinistic, it is not so intended. But the facts are that in most American households, there is a certain division of labor and responsibilities. This division is more or less traditional, and quite frankly, it's a waste of time to ignore it. If you follow my advice below, you'll get through to more decision makers this way than if you do it any other way.

1) Where the phone is listed in the man's name, ask for the man IF:

   a) Your product or service has to do with the structure of the house, the outside of the house, or any of the major systems, such as heating, air conditioning, or insulation.

   b) You deal in financial services such as investments or life insurance.

2) Where the phone is listed by initial only, assume a female head of household but qualify. Some men, such as Alfonse Theodorakis Jones, will be listed as A. T. Jones. Frankly, women are well advised not to list their first names since this encourages crank calls. Our only interest is in determining whether A. T. is the buyer or not.

Here's how your script goes for calling A. T. Jones:

YOU: *Ring, ring.*

WOMAN'S VOICE: Hello.

YOU: Is this Ms. Jones?

WOMAN'S VOICE: Yes, it is.

YOU: Ms. Jones, this is Fred Smithers with Acme Insurance. Tell me, do you take care of the financial decisions for your family?

MS. JONES: Yes, I do.

3) If your product involves the inside of the home, its decoration, cleanliness (carpets, drapes), education (books, subscriptions), or other service providers, ask for the woman of the house. In test marketing our dental program, we found that our buyer was Mrs. Jones.

4) Here's the wild card. Many female heads of households are divorcées or widows. For reasons of safety, they have left the phone listed in the man's name. So if you call and ask for "Mr. Jones," you may occasionally hear a recent widow respond, "He just died." But after they have had time to collect themselves a much more common answer from a divorcée or widow is, "He's not in." Or even more strongly, "Who's calling?"

Here's your rule: As above, when the phone is listed in a man's name, ask for the man. But if the woman says, "He's not in," or "Who's calling?" immediately qualify with:

Is this Ms. Jones? Ms. Jones, this is Fred Smithers with Acme Company. Do you take care of the _____ decisions for your family?

Assignment: As needed, write several questions to determine authority to buy. You may need now to go back and rewrite your introduction.

SAMPLE SCRIPTS

On the pages that follow, I'll give you complete scripts for the four examples we've been developing so far as well as for several other products or services. I have also included a First Call Script Development Form. As you study these, please keep in mind that it is impossible to give an example of every type of product for which you can prospect with this style. Just find the one closest to what you do and rewrite.

Tax-Free Bond Fund

Comment: Please note the open-ended fallback. Where you have many products you could sell, try this type of fallback.

INTRO: May I speak with M/M _____, please? Very good. M/M _____, this is _____ with (COMPANY), members of the New York Stock Exchange. You know who we are, don't you?

If No: Stocks, Bonds, Wall Street. Does that ring a bell?

OFFER: I have some important information on what is called a tax-free municipal bond fund. Have you ever heard of one of these before?

BENEFIT/INTEREST:

Yes or No: Basically, as you know, it's a portfolio of top quality tax-free municipal bonds. These have been selected both for income and safety. Could I send you some information on it?

NOT INTERESTED AT ALL: Thankyouverymuch.

QUALIFICATION: Very good. I will get it out to you right away. If I send it out to you (TODAY/TOMORROW), you should receive it by (DAY). Will you have time to look it over by (DAY)? (RESPONSE) If you do like the idea, would an investment of $_____ be a problem to you at this particular time? (RESPONSE)

QUALIFIES: (Are these funds available now?) Just one other question and I'll let you go. In case I can't get in touch with you during the (DAY/EVENING), how can I reach you during the (DAY/EVENING)? I have your address down as _____. Is that correct? Great! Haveagoodday and thankyouverymuch.

DOES NOT QUALIFY: Is this just a temporary condition or do you have any monies coming due in the next six months? (RESPONSE) Very good. Suppose I get back to you in (MONTH), okay?

FALLBACK: Just one quick question. What kind of investments have you been making lately? (RESPONSE) Great! If I came up with an idea in (FIELD HE OR SHE MENTIONED), you wouldn't mind if I called you back and mentioned it to you, would you? (RESPONSE) One last question and I'll let you go. In case I can't catch up with you during the (DAY/EVENING), how can I reach you during the (DAY/EVENING)?

Bank CD

INTRO: May I speak with M/M _____, please? Very good. M/M _____, this is _____ with (BANK NAME). You know who we are, don't you?

If No: We're the bank that specializes in _____. Does that ring a bell?

OFFER/BENEFIT/INTEREST:

M/M _____, I have some very important information for you on a guaranteed investment. It's a bank CD and it's paying _____ percent. Could I send you some information on our terms and rates?

NOT INTERESTED AT ALL: Thankyouverymuch.

QUALIFICATION: Very good. I will get it out to you right away. If I send it out to you (TODAY/TOMORROW), you should receive it by (DAY)? Will you have time to look it over by (DAY)? (RESPONSE) If you like what you read, how much would you be planning to invest? (RESPONSE)

> **QUALIFIES:** (Are these funds available now?) Just one other question and I'll let you go. In case I can't get in touch with you during the (DAY/EVENING), how can I reach you during the (DAY/EVENING)? I have your address down as _____. Is that correct? Great! Haveagoodday and thankyouverymuch.

> **DOES NOT QUALIFY:** When, over the next year, will your CD's and T-Bills be maturing? (RESPONSE) Suppose I get back to you in (MONTH) and you can give us the once over, then, Okay?

FALLBACK: Just one quick question. We have a fantastic loan package right now that lets you borrow on the equity in your home. Is this something you might like to have on reserve in case you need some money in a hurry? (RESPONSE) IF YES: Very good. Let me put some information in the mail to you and I'll check back with you in a week to see if you have some questions, fair enough?

Commercial Real Estate—Apartment Building Owner

Comment: Some lists, such as owners of apartment buildings, are very easy to get. Especially in major cities, lots of commercial agents get the same list and pound the phones. The problem is that some prospects get so many predictable calls, they really don't want to hear another. So our tactic is one of reversal. To get them to listen, we reverse the typical offer. For instance, there is no shortage of good buyers for apartment buildings. There is a shortage of good properties for sale. Most brokers, following the obvious path, call and look for people who want to sell. But the owners have heard it ten thousand times before. You need something to get their attention. So instead of making a call to try and get a listing on an apartment building, *we'll try and sell one to someone who already owns one.* (After all, the best prospect to buy an apartment building is someone who already owns one.) Then, if he is not interested in picking up another building, we're at least in communication with him and can find out his plans for selling the one he has. For those of you in another market, you should use a reversal if you are in a highly competitive market that is heavily telephone prospected. By the way, the reason I have not used the usual "You know who we are, don't you?" questions below is that when the prospect in this heavily prospected market even hears that you are from a commercial real estate office, the "I'm not interested" reflex comes into play. We at least want a chance for fifteen seconds. So grab it with an approach that is quite different from one he or she has heard before.

OFFER/BENEFIT/INTEREST:

May I speak with M/M _____, please? Very good. M/M _____, this is _____ with (COMPANY). I have some information available on an eight-unit apartment building we have for sale. I'm calling to find out if you have given any thought at all to increasing your real estate holdings and possibly even becoming rich? (*If Negative:* You're rich already then, right?)

NOT INTERESTED AT ALL: Thankyouverymuch.

QUALIFICATION: Great! Let me ask you this. If you were to get another building, would you want to sell some property or would you plan to use some new money? The building I have in mind would require a downpayment in the range of $_____. If you did like it, would $_____ be a problem to you at this particular time? (RESPONSE) Let me send you some information on this one and get back in touch with you in a couple of days, okay?

> ### QUALIFIES: (RESPONSE) Very good. In case I can't get in touch with you during the (DAY/EVENING), how can I reach you during the (DAY/EVENING)? (RESPONSE) Very good. I will drop this in the mail right away and then talk to you, say, on (DAY), fair enough?

DOES NOT QUALIFY: GO TO FALLBACK TO CHECK ON LISTING PROPERTY

FALLBACK:

By the way, what are your plans for your building on (ADDRESS)?

What would have to happen for you to be interested in selling it?

Interested in Selling: What I would like to do is set up a time to get the information so we can give you an up-to-date estimate of what your property might sell for in today's market. I have a spot available on (DAY) at (TIME). I am also free on (DAY) at (TIME). Which of those would be better for you?

Variable/Universal Life

Comment: Here, if the prospect is not interested in variable or universal life, our fallback is to check on the prospect's home-owner and auto insurance and find what's called the X-date—the policy expiration date. Another possible fallback would be to find the person's birthdate since that determines when rates go up. This script can be used for a variable or a universal policy as the benefits of each are basically the same.

OFFER/BENEFIT/INTEREST:

May I speak with M/M _____, please? Very good. M/M _____, this is _____ with (COMPANY). You know who we are, don't you?

I have some important information on how to get a higher rate of return on your money than a CD. The interest compounds. Uncle Sam doesn't touch it at tax time. And if something should happen to you, your family would get a whole bunch of money. Could I send you some information on it?

QUALIFICATION: Very good. I will get it out to you right away. If I send it out to you (TODAY/TOMORROW), you should receive it by (DAY). Will you have time to look it over by (DAY)? (RESPONSE) If you were to decide to increase your savings, how much could you set aside on a monthly basis? (RESPONSE) One last question and I'll let you go. If you do like what you read, is there any reason why you wouldn't want to get together so I could show you how much money you could make on this? (RESPONSE) Very good. I'll give you a call back, say, on (DAY) and we'll see where we go from there, fair enough?

FALLBACK: Just one quick question and I'll let you go. Right now, (COMPANY) is extremely competitive on our auto and home-owner policies. Tell me, am I too early or too late to give you a quote on your homeowner insurance? (RESPONSE) In what month does your policy expire? (RESPONSE)

> **EXPIRES SOON:** Okay. M/M _____, what I would like to do is drop by, work up a quick quote for you, and just leave it with you. I have to be in (NAME OF AREA) on (DAY). I have a spot open at (TIME) and again at (TIME). Which of those would be better for you?

> **EXPIRES LATER:** Okay. Suppose I get back to you in (MONTH) and work up a quote for you then, okay? By the way, when do you pay premiums on your auto insurance again? And who carries it currently?

> **AUTO EXPIRES SOON:** Okay. M/M _____, what I would like to do is drop by, work up a quick quote for you, and just leave it with you. I have to be in (NAME OF AREA) on (DAY). I have a spot open at (TIME) and again at (TIME). Which of those would be better for you?

> **AUTO EXPIRES LATER:** Very good. I will give you a call on your auto insurance in (MONTH). We'll get together then, okay?

Cellular Phone

INTRO: May I speak with M/M _____, please? Very good. M/M _____, this is _____ with _____. Does the name _____ ring a bell?

IF NO: We're the division of _____ putting phones in cars.

OFFER: M/M _____, I have some very interesting information for you on how our cellular phone can save you time, money, and possibly keep you out of trouble with your (HUSBAND/WIFE) if you're going to be late. Could I send it to you?

NOT INTERESTED AT ALL: Thankyouverymuch.

QUALIFICATION: Very good. I will get it out to you right away. If I send it out today, you should receive it by (DAY). Would you have time to look it over by (DAY)? Very good. Normally, what is the best time of day to reach you? And what is your direct extension number? Very good. One last question and I'll let you go. Depending on the model, these phones will lease for anywhere from $_____ to $_____ per month. I don't imagine that amount would be a problem for you, would it?

> **DOES QUALIFY:** Suppose I give you a call on (DAY) about (TIME) and we'll get a better idea of whether what we have is what you need, fair enough?

> **DOES NOT QUALIFY:** When should I get back to you?

MULTILEVEL MARKETING DISTRIBUTORS

INTRO: May I speak with M/M _____, please? Very good. M/M _____, my name is _____. I'm a direct distributor for _____. I'm sure you know who we are, don't you?

OFFER: M/M _____, we specialize in two things. Household cleaning products and helping people make money, part-time. Could I send you some information on how we might help you, or someone else in your family, pick up some extra money part-time?

QUALIFICATION: I will get it out right away. Just a couple of quick questions. How much extra are you looking for? And how much time do you figure you could devote to that a week? One last question and I'll let you go. To make money, you have to be willing to spend some. If you did like the idea, an initial investment of $_____ is required. Would that amount be a problem for you at this particular time?

DOES QUALIFY: Great! I'll send this off to you and get back to you next week to see if you have any questions. Fair enough?

FALLBACK: Just one quick question and I'll let you go. I know you use a lot of the type of products we sell. May I put a catalog in the mail and then check back with you from time to time?

SCRIPT DEVELOPMENT FORM:

Comment: Type out a form as shown below on regular-sized typing paper. Make lots of copies. Use key words and phrases I have inserted to help get your thinking process going. And then do lots of rewriting. Take it one section at a time. Good luck.

INTRO: May I speak with M/M _____, please? Very good. M/M _____, this is _____ with (COMPANY). You know who we are, don't you?

If No: We're the _____

_____

Does that ring a bell?

OFFER: I have some important information on _____

_____

BENEFIT: _____

_____

INTEREST: Could I send you some information on it?

NOT INTERESTED AT ALL: Thankyouverymuch.

QUALIFICATION: Very good. I will get it out to you right away. If I send it out to you (TODAY/TOMORROW), you should receive it by (DAY). Will you have time to look it over by (DAY)? (RESPONSE) If you do like the idea, (ASK FOR MONEY) _____

_____

QUALIFIES: Just one other question and I'll let you go.

_____

_____

I have your address down as _____. Is that correct? Great! Haveagoodday and thankyouverymuch.

DOES NOT QUALIFY: _____

_____

(RESPONSE) Very good. Suppose I get back to you in (MONTH). Okay?

FALLBACK: Just one quick question. _____

_____
_____
_____ ?

5

Script Writing—Part II: Appointment Scripts

Very probably, you have read or heard about the spiraling amounts of money that it costs American corporations to send their salespeople on even one face-to-face appointment. It's for this reason that it is especially important to qualify before you go.

Certainly one way to do this is to qualify on a first call, send some information and allow some time for it to sink in, make a second call, *and then* set the appointment. Another way to do it is to set an appointment on the first call but only *after* asking detailed questions to determine both interest and qualification.

MYSTERY APPOINTMENTS

Before getting into the techniques on designing appointment scripts, I do want to take a couple of shots at a type of appointment setting I find particularly objectionable. It is practiced in many industries. I call it the mystery appointment. If it sounds bizarre as you read on, trust me. This is the way many major firms teach their salespeople to prospect.

In setting a mystery appointment, you don't let the prospect know anything more than your name, your company, and that you have some important but unspecified need to see him or her right away. Basically, you just bully your way in the door. Those who work for the offending companies will recognize this style instantly.

M/M _____, this is Joe Dokes with Acme Company. I have a few new ideas which I'd like to share with you. I'm going to be in your neighborhood between four and six o'clock on Friday. Which of those would be better for you?

Another version is practiced extensively by multilevel marketing companies whose distributors are explicitly told not to tell a prospective distributor *anything about the meeting.* Here's how one of these might go. (And this is for calling your friends!)

FRED: Jack, it's your old fishing buddy, Fred.

JACK: Hey, when we going?

FRED: I got some place else I want to take you and Alice.

JACK: What you got it in mind?

FRED: It's something I think will be very important for you and Alice. Suppose I pick you both up at seven o'clock Thursday evening.

JACK: What are we going to do?

FRED: That's exactly what I'm going to show you. Thursday at seven?

JACK: Yeah, I guess.

FRED: Great! Thursday at seven. See you then.

One multilevel distributor I know went to pick up "Jack," found all the lights on, the TV on, dinner on the table, and no one home. I wonder why.

Here's a promise. If you trick your friends and prospects into seeing you, you'll come to hate your job. Remember that. And don't set mystery appointments. Instead, take on faith, for now, that in the time you spend driving out to see one of these mystery leads—or anyone else you have forced yourself on—you can sit down at the phone, find five or ten excellent prospects, and set some quality appointments. So no bully tactics. And no mystery, please.

SECOND CALL APPOINTMENT SCRIPTS

Let's start with the second call appointment. It's an easier script to develop because you really already have a foot in the door because of last week's qualification call. However, we first have to handle a problem with second calls.

The Second Call Problem:

Here's the second call problem. Last week you sent some information. This week you call back. Here goes the all-too-typical second call.

FRED: Jack, it's Fred Smithers over here at Acme. How are you?

JACK: Fine.

FRED: I sent you that information last week. Did you get it?

JACK: Doesn't ring a bell.

FRED: Remember the big package? Brown envelope?

JACK: Oh, yes. I've got it. Haven't had time to look at it yet. It's about number six down from the top.

FRED: When do you think you'll have time to look at it?

JACK: Try me next week some time.

Let's do a triple whammy handle on the "I didn't get it/I didn't read it" problem. You'll probably never stamp it out entirely. But we sure can cut down on it. Here's what we'll do.

1) Mutilate the material you send out. By "mutilate" I mean write all over it, circle items, draw arrows, and so forth. If you do this, I promise you, your prospect is far more likely to read it.

2) Instead of sending a hand-written note, only write what you can put on the back of your business card. Take your business card,

flip it around, upside down and backwards, and write on the back, "Here's the information I promised." And then sign only your *first* name. Then, using a paperclip, attach the card to the mutilated material.

When the information arrives, the prospect will open the envelope, see your first name on the back of the card, won't have a clue who you are, will then have to take the card off, read that, and then, staring him in the face in his other hand is your written material with phrases like, "Read This," "See Page 9" in black or some other prominent color. The prospect will now read what you've highlighted and perhaps the rest. Plus, by forcing your prospect to get physically involved with your business card, you've had the opportunity again to let him or her know who you are.

Remember, you didn't send the prospect information because you care if he or she reads it. You needed to send it in order to establish who you are and to prove *through your actions* that you're not a high-pressure salesperson.

PARTS OF THE SECOND CALL

Like the qualification script, your second call appointment script is made up of distinct parts. We'll go over them one at a time. Then I'll give you several examples of second call scripts and finally, a Second Call Script Development Form.

As you did in the chapter on qualification scripts, you should adapt what you read to your own product or market and rewrite the script examples many times until they exactly fit you.

1) Intro and bypass

By "bypass" I refer to the technique whereby we ignore completely whether the prospect received or read the material sent. Here's how you do it:

May I speak with M/M _____, please? M/M _____ this is _____ with (COMPANY). I sent you that information last week but before I recommend you get involved there are two or three points I would like to go over with you. Do you have a moment or two?

Please note: I didn't even remind the prospect what the information was on. And I really don't care if the prospect remembers getting it or not. All I care about is the fact that by accepting the material from me, the prospect is now obligated to discuss it. With the intro and bypass in place at the very beginning of the second call, you should really hear no more of the "I didn't get it/I didn't read it."

A note of warning: Please don't expect everyone you qualified on first calls last week to set an appointment for this week. Here are some very broad rules of thumb that you can apply. Expect about twenty percent of the people you talk to to be too busy right at the end of your intro. Expect another twenty to thirty percent to blow away before you get to your appointment close. And finally, if you do it right, you should be getting appointments with fifty to sixty percent of last week's cherries.

2) Sell yourself or your company

If you work for a very well-known company, an IBM, a Merrill Lynch, a Bank of America, you don't need to spend any time at all telling your prospect about your company. These companies do an extraordinary job of doing that for you. But suppose you work for Armadillo Computers. You've got a real problem. You'd better take a moment and tell people who the company is. Or, if you work for a well-known company, take a moment, and at this point, *sell yourself.*

Frankly, I learned of this principle when I first started my business. My practice was to go out on a sales presentation, make the presentation, and then go directly to a coffee shop and sit down and analyze what I had done. A number of patterns began to emerge. One of them was that when I would get down near the close, the prospect would say, "Who are you again?" And I would have to present my credentials all over again.

So I began experimenting with different points in my sales presentation to present my credentials. The best place seemed to be at the very beginning of my sales presentation. I've watched a number of great salespeople in action, and they all instinctively seem to do it right at the beginning.

Here's how I did it when I started my company and how I do it now when I am dealing with someone who may not know who I am or what my company does:

> Mr. Jones, let me tell you just a little bit about who we are and what we do. The name of the company again is Telephone Marketing, Inc. My name is Bill Good. We specialize in training salespeople to find new business by phone; and in your industry, we've worked with such people as _____, _____, and _____. I would imagine that if you did get interested in one of our seminars, you would want to check with some of the other people in your industry that have used us, is that correct?

They always want to check references. So I tell them they should. I even insist they write down the names and phone numbers of people who have given me their permission to use them as referrals. What kind of credibility do you think I earn with that?

Here's a self-introduction that we recommend for stockbrokers.

> Since we've never met, I'd like to tell you a little about myself and the kind of work I do. My name, again, is _____. I specialize in (PRODUCT SENT), tax-advantaged investments, and retirement planning. I'll answer any questions you have and stay in touch with new ideas and needed information. But I recognize that you're probably busy, and I'll respect that by keeping my calls brief and to the point. Does that sound fair enough to you, M/M _____?

Remember: People like doing business with people they know. Since you never have been introduced, let's now take care of that. In reality, a salesperson with, say, one hundred accounts has one hundred part-time jobs. If you were in fact applying for a part-time job, you would of course tell something about yourself. So let's do it here as well. Its effect is unbelievable.

Also, the "sell yourself or company" step is very important to establish a professional image. You'll need this image to get your prospect to answer detailed and sometimes very personal questions. If you go into a doctor's office, you'll see professionalism at work. They've got it down to the point that they will give a new patient a questionnaire to fill out, and people will actually tell a complete stranger about family histories of insanity, vile and loathsome diseases, and strange sexual practices. And all because they perceive the person in the white coat to be a professional! Not bad.

I should point out that with the sell yourself step, we are making the leap from prospecting skills to selling skills. In this section, we've begun using a sales technique called assumptive selling. We have begun to act as if the sale has already occurred. Reread the broker self-introduction on page 82. You'll see what I mean.

One Old Schooler wrote a book and said, "The sale begins when the customer says no." I would say, "The sale really begins with the sell yourself step." While this is not a book on sales technique, we do need at least to begin using some sales ideas from this point forward in our presentation. It's from this point forward that we begin acting less like a prospector who is discarding dirt and more like a gold refiner who is making sure he or she doesn't lose a speck. This is not an open sesame to begin pit polishing. Just begin to shift your point of view from discard to keep.

Assignment: Using the examples provided as models, rewrite your own self-introduction or company introduction. When complete, it should not take more than thirty seconds to deliver.

3) Bridge to questionnaire

After your introduction, you'll need a transition to get smoothly into the questions you'll be asking. Here's a bridge to questionnaire as we've used it in the securities industry. Please note once again the assumptive selling techniques. I've underlined the key passages.

> For me to do a good job for you <u>over time,</u> I'll really need to know more about where you are financially, how you got that way, but most importantly, where you want to be in the future. <u>We can do that one of two ways.</u> We can set up a time to get together, or I can run some questions by you right now. <u>How would you like to proceed from here?</u>

Here's how you might do it if you were a car dealer and you have a crew of prospectors working for you to get people into the show room.

M/M _____, to make sure our new Thundermobile is exactly the right car for you, there are some questions I would like to run by you. We can do that in one of two ways. You can set up a time to come down to the showroom, or I can spend a few minutes by phone with you right now. Which way would you like to proceed from here?

4) The questionnaire

The guts of the second call appointment script is the questionnaire. Since there are thousands of products that can be sold and tens of millions of questions that can be asked, it is very difficult in this section to do any more than give several examples of questionnaires and to give several broad rules that apply.

First, the rules:

1) The first two or three questions should be null questions. A null question is any question the answer to which doesn't matter. It simply gets the prospect answering questions.

Examples:

A) Let me just make sure I have your address correct. I have you down at 405 South Main Street, is that correct?

B) And your position is: Vice-President, Materials Acquisition, correct?

C) And normally, what's the best time of day to reach you?

As you can see, no one of these questions is critical, but each does play a role in getting the person into a flow of question answering. The pattern you want to establish is: You ask, they answer.

2) Ask less personal or less confidential questions first.

Call it the salami technique if you want. We just take a small slice at a time rather than going for the whole thing. If you try and grab the whole sausage, people will resist. Just ask for a little bit at a time.

Here are some examples of questionnaires from the securities, insurance, and commercial real estate industries, and how I might design one for an automobile dealership.

Please note in question 3a below I am qualifying *again*. I did it on the first call. Now I'm going to make certain my prospect has some M O N E Y. Sometimes prospects will tell you on the first call that they have money but it may not be available RIGHT NOW when you make the second call. That's why it never hurts to requalify.

SECURITIES INDUSTRY SECOND CALL QUESTIONNAIRE

0) Normally would you prefer information sent to your home or office?

00) What is the best time of day to get hold of you?

1. a) How would you describe your investment philosophy?

   b) Based on your past performance, on a scale of one to ten, how would you rate your abilities as an investor?

2. a) Have you ever had any outstanding investments?

   b) Have you ever lost a lot of money on an investment before?

3. If you wanted to raise $_____ for an investment, how long would it take?

   a) Occasionally we get some extremely attractive investments that require a minimum investment of $_____. If one of these came along, would that be a problem for you?

   (IF PROBLEM) If it were something you *really did like,* what is the *most* you could conceivably come up with?

   b) How much do you expect to have available within the next twelve months in the way of new investable funds? Where is it coming from?

   c) What about CD's? When will they be expiring in the next year?

   d) Normally, what kind of balances do you keep in your money market funds and checking accounts?

4. Have you ever bought (PRODUCT SENT)? (IF YES) What do you (LIKE, NOT LIKE) about it?

5. Just a couple of other questions here. How far are you from retirement age?

6. (IF RETIRED, GO TO 7) At what after-tax rate of return are your investments going to have to grow in order to meet the retirement

objectives that you've set for yourself? What inflation rate have you factored in?

7. (IF RETIRED) What after-tax rate of return do your investments have to yield in order to maintain your current lifestyle?

By the way, this questionnaire is not the longest I have ever designed. Probably just the best. Like most salespeople who have seen this for the first time, you probably don't think there is a chance in the world people would answer it. What can I say? You can die a disbeliever, or you can give it, or its equivalent for your industry, a try. Your success with a questionnaire such as this depends only on your having previously been accepted as a professional *and* on delivering the questionnaire in a relaxed, easy style.

Here's a much, much shorter questionnaire.

INSURANCE INDUSTRY SECOND CALL QUESTIONNAIRE

1) What are your savings goals, say, twenty years from now?

2) Have you worked out how much you need to set aside in order to achieve that?

3) At what rate do your investments have to grow in order to meet the retirement objectives you've set for yourself?

And if I were to get a call from Lee Iacocca, here's how I might design a second call questionnaire form for Chrysler.

AUTOMOBILE SECOND CALL QUESTIONNAIRE

1) What do you most want in an automobile?

2) How many in your family?

3) Who would be the main driver?

4) Were you planning to trade in your current car?

   IF NO: What kind of financing did you have in mind?

5) If you were really excited about, say, our _____ model, what's the most you figure you could handle on a montly payment?

Assignment: First write down as many questions as you can think of that could be asked. Then arrange these in order from least personal to most personal. Keep rewriting until you are happy.

5) **The close**

The close for the appointment is actually quite easy. If you've done a good questionnaire, the questions have worked some magic on the prospect's mind. They've actually created interest. And so we really don't need too many techniques for closing for an appointment. Generally, we just ask the prospect if he or she would like to get together and talk about it, and the answer will generally be "Sure."

However, we do want to be just a little bit more elaborate than this. So we'll use a *closing formula* I call the ABC close. You can use the ABC closing formula to close for anything. But here, our interest is in getting an appointment with a qualified and interested prospect. (By the way, some Old School sales trainers used the phrase ABC to indicate "Always Be Closing." I think this is junk. The close is simply that part of a sales presentation that asks for a commitment to act. The entire presentation is not made up of closing as this statement indicates.) Here's what the ABC close is all about:

A = Action. A close always involves an action. You don't want the prospect to just *think* about anything. You want him or her to *do something.* So on the first step of our close, we'll recommend an action.

Here are some examples of ACTION steps:

> Mr. Jones, I think it would be an excellent idea if you brought your last two years' tax returns down to my office.

> Mrs. Smithers, why don't you pull together all of your insurance policies?

Or, to your teenage daughter,

> Nicci, I think it would be an excellent idea if you cleaned up your room now.

B = Benefit. To make certain no good prospects get away at this point, stress a benefit for taking the action you have just recommended.

Here are some benefits for taking the actions recommended above. I have put the benefits in **boldface.**

87

Mr. Jones, I think it would be an excellent idea if you brought your last two years' tax returns down to my office. **I am sure I can show you a way to cut your taxes *significantly.***

Mrs. Smithers, why don't you pull together all of your insurance policies? **There's an excellent chance I can show you how to get more coverage for the same amount you're now paying.**

Nicci, I think it would be an excellent idea if you cleaned up your room now. **By doing that now, you have a chance of at least seeing daylight next weekend.**

C = Commitment. After you've told the prospect what you want him or her to do and have given a good reason for doing it, go immediately, without pause, without passing go, without collecting $200, to the commitment question.

Here are some complete closes with the commitment question in **boldface.**

Mr. Jones, I think it would be an excellent idea if you brought your last two years' tax returns down to my office. I am sure I can show you a way to cut your taxes significantly. **I have a spot in my calendar on Thursday at four and I'm also free Friday morning at ten. Which of those would be better for you?**

Mrs. Smithers, why don't you pull together all of your insurance policies? There's an excellent chance I can show you how to get more coverage for the same amount you're now paying. **I have to be out your way next Wednesday evening. I have a time available at six-thirty and again at eight-thirty. Which looks best to you?**

Nicci, I think it would be an excellent idea if you cleaned up your room now. By doing that now, you have a chance of at least seeing daylight next weekend. **Would you like to start now or in thirty seconds?**

6) After the close

The appointment's closed. Now let's really firm it up. You can do this with a number of simple questions, as follows:

1) I have your address as 405 Framitz Street, is that correct?

2) What is the nearest major cross street?

3) Do you have a pencil handy? My name again is Fred Smithers. My phone number is 333-4444. If there is any problem with three o'clock next Thursday, you'll give me a call, won't you?

4) Very good. I'll see you next Thursday, and you have a nice day, okay?

That takes care of the script parts of a second call. Here are some examples of complete second call scripts and then a Second Call Script Development Form.

Cellular Phone

INTRO & BYPASS: May I speak with M/M _____, please? M/M _____, this is _____ with _____. I sent you that information on our cellular phone, but before I recommend that you go the next step and get a demonstration, let me check over several points with you. Do you have a moment or two?

SELL COMPANY: First of all, let me tell you a little bit about who we are. We are a division of _____ which has been specializing in communications equipment almost since the telephone was invented. We've installed cellular phones for companies like _____, _____, and _____. I would imagine you would want to check with some of the people in your industry before going ahead with us, is that correct? I will be happy to give you names of people to call.

BRIDGE TO QUESTIONNAIRE: One other thing I should tell you. We won't sell you a cellular phone unless we feel it's something you'll benefit from. So let me take just a moment of your time and run some questions by you.

QUESTIONNAIRE:

1) First of all, have you ever used a car phone before?
2) How much time do you spend getting to and from work each day?
3) What other travel time do you have?
4) What business could you actually do in your car that would more than pay a few modest dollars for your phone?

ABC CLOSE: M/M _____, you know what you ought to do? (RESPONSE) You ought to actually make a few calls with one of our phones and see for yourself how it works. This way, you can get an excellent idea of how exactly you might be able to justify it. One of our account representatives will be in (NAME OF AREA) on (DAY) and (DAY). He actually has a phone in his car he will let you use. He has a spot on (DAY) at (TIME) and another one on (DAY) at (TIME). Which of those would be better for you?

AFTER THE CLOSE:

1) I have your address as _____, is that correct?
2) What is the nearest major cross street?
3) Do you have a pencil handy? My name again is _____. My phone number is _____. If there is any problem with (TIME) next (DAY), you'll give me a call, won't you?
4) Very good. We'll see you next (DAY), and you have a nice day, okay?

Comment: This script is written for someone who is setting appointments for another. Most any script can be adapted to do this.

REAL ESTATE INVESTOR

INTRO & BYPASS: Hi! This is _____ over here at _____. I spoke to you last week and you wanted me to check out some properties for you in (NAME OF AREA). I found something I think you will be very interested in, but before I recommend we go ahead, there are two or three points I would like to check over with you. Do you have a second?

SELL SELF: First of all, I would like to tell you just a bit more about myself and the kind of work I do. I specialize in only one kind of property, and that's apartment buildings. I don't sell houses. I don't sell raw land. And I don't sell office buildings. And I'm in no particular hurry to find a building for you, especially one that's not right for you. Does this sound like the kind of person you could conceivably do business with?

BRIDGE TO QUESTIONNAIRE: For me to do a good job for you over time, I will need to know exactly what you are looking for. I have a number of buildings in mind, but I need to check some points with you first. We can do that now or we can set up a time to get together and we'll do it while we're driving around to see several buildings currently on the market. Which way would you like to proceed from here?

QUESTIONNAIRE:

1) If you did decide to buy a building, would your main motivation be shelter or income?
2) What income properties do you currently own? And when did you buy it/them?
3) I would imagine that you would want to manage these yourself rather than hire someone to do it for you, is that correct?
4) To raise a downpayment in the range of $_____, would you need to liquidate another property or could you just write a check?
5) What is the most you could carry now in the way of a negative cash flow?

ABC CLOSE: Very good. Here's how we work. We first get together here at the office and look over the photos, rents, prices, costs, and so forth. We also go over the tax and wealth building implications of owning buildings and see if that is really the direction that is right for you at this time. If all systems are go, we drive by those you like. So—what would be the best time during the week for us to get together? (RESPONSE) Very good. I have a spot open on (DAY) at (TIME) or (TIME). Which of those would be better for you?

AFTER THE CLOSE:

1) Do you have a pencil handy? My name again is _____. My phone number is _____.
2) Our office is located here at _____. Do you know where that is?
3) (Give directions as necessary.)
4) If there is any problem with (DAY) at (TIME), will you give me a call?
5) Very good. I'll see you then on (DAY). You have a good one.

Life Insurance

INTRO & BYPASS: May I speak with M/M _____, please? Very good. M/M _____, this is _____ with _____. I sent you that information last week, but before I recommend you get involved, there are two or three points I would like to go over with you. Do you have a moment or two?

SELL SELF: Since we've never met, I would like to take a moment and tell you a little about myself and the kind of work I do. When we meet, you will notice I am in my twenties, early twenties. And you may certainly wonder why someone who looks like they just got out of high school should be making recommendations that could affect the rest of your life. Well, let me tell you this. I can promise you two things. The company has been here a lot longer than I have, and second, if I don't know the answer to something, I'll certainly find someone who will. Does that sound fair enough to you?

BRIDGE TO QUESTIONNAIRE: For me to do a good job for you over time, there are some things I need to know about where you are financially, how you got that way, but most importantly, where you want to be in the future. We can do that one of two ways. You can come down here to my office or I can come visit you. Which way would you like to proceed from here?

NO GO ON APPOINTMENT: Just one quick question and I'll let you go. Right now, _____ is extremely competitive on our homeowner insurance. Tell me, am I too early or too late to give you a quote? (RESPONSE) In what month does your policy expire?

EXPIRES SOON: Okay. M/M _____, what I would like to do is drop by, work up a quick quote for you, and just leave it with you. I have to be in (NAME OF AREA) on (DAY). I have a spot open at (TIME) and again at (TIME). Which of those would be better for you?

EXPIRES LATER: Okay. Suppose I get back to you in (MONTH) and work up a quote for you then, okay? By the way, when do you pay premiums on your auto insurance again? And who carries it currently?

AUTO EXPIRES SOON: Okay. M/M _____, what I would like to do is drop by, work up a quick quote for you, and just leave it with you. I have to be in (NAME OF AREA) on (DAY). I have a spot open at (TIME) and again at (TIME). Which of those would be better for you?

AUTO EXPIRES LATER: Very good. I will give you a call on your auto insurance in (MONTH). We'll get together then, okay?

Comment: This script was written for a salesman who was twenty-three at the time and looked about seventeen. When he would go into people's houses, their jaws would hit the floor. The principle here is: Handle obvious liabilities as early as possible *and you bring them up first.* You will also note that I went directly for the appointment at the end of the Bridge to Questionnaire. Why? It felt right. Also note that I built a fallback into my second call script. As you progress in your script writing skills, you will see that you can definitely "mix and match" script parts.

SECOND CALL APPOINTMENT SCRIPT DEVELOPMENT FORM

INTRO: May I speak with M/M _____, please? Very good. M/M _____, this is _____ with (COMPANY). I sent you that information last week, but before I recommend you get involved, there are two or three points I would like to go over with you. Do you have a moment or two?

SELL SELF/COMPANY: Since we've never met, let me tell you a little bit about (myself/my company) and the kind of work we do. First of all, (my/the company) name again is _____. Basically, I/we specialize in

_____

_____

I'll answer any questions you have and stay in touch with new ideas and needed information. But I recognize that you're probably busy, and I'll respect that by keeping my calls brief and to the point. Does that sound fair enough to you, M/M _____?

BRIDGE TO QUESTIONNAIRE: For me to do a good job for you *over time,* I'll really need to know more about _____

_____

We can do that one of two ways. We can set up a time to get together, or I can run some questions by you right now. *How would you like to proceed from here?*

QUESTIONNAIRE:

_____
_____
_____
_____
_____
_____
_____
_____

ABC CLOSE: M/M _____, I suggest that we (ACTION) _____
_____

I can (BENEFIT) _____
_____

I have a spot open in my calendar on (DAY) at (TIME). I am also free on (DAY) at (TIME). Which of those would be better for you?

AFTER THE CLOSE:

1) I have your address as _____, is that correct?
2) What is the nearest major cross street?
3) Do you have a pencil handy? My name again is _____. My phone number is _____. If there is any problem with _____ next Thursday, you'll give me a call, won't you?
4) Very good. I'll see you next (DAY), and you have a nice day, okay?

ASSIGNMENT: Using your script-rewriting skills, rewrite a script for a second call appointment.

FIRST CALL APPOINTMENT SCRIPTS

There are quite obviously some similarities between a Second Call Appointment Script and a First Call Appointment Script. However, I should point out that unless you are selling something truly unique, well known, or in great demand, you may find it difficult to set appointments on first calls. This is certainly not to say it can't be done. It can. But do keep in mind that if you run into stiff resistance on your first call, drop back to the qualification script and run a two-call approach.

In this section, we'll walk through the parts of the first call appointment script, give examples of each, give some examples of completed scripts, and then provide you with a Script Development Form that will help you create your own script.

1) The Intro

[This section is identical to the intro in the qualification script.]

May I speak with M/M _____, please? Very good. M/M _____, this is _____ with (COMPANY). You know who we are, don't you? (Or, Can you hear me okay on this phone? Or, Does the name _____ ring a bell?)

2) Reason for the Call

Here's where you make or break your First Call Appointment Script. You really *do* need a good reason to call. "I'm going to be in your neighborhood," doesn't cut it. Who cares where you're going to be? Instead, consider the following possibilities as reasons for your call:

PRICE CHANGE.

If your price is going up, or has just come down, you can certainly call and tell them. For instance, you might be selling computers. A reason for the call, in the event of a price change, might go like this:

M/M _____, I'm calling to let you know that the price of our Armadillo Computer is going to go up in two weeks.

Or, if prices have dropped, you can call and say:

M/M _____, that Armadillo PC you've been thinking about has just come down in price.

NEW PRODUCT OR CHANGE OF PRODUCT INFORMATION.

If there is any change in a feature or benefit of a product, call and tell people about it. For example, suppose you are a residen-

95

tial real estate agent. You may have a particularly desirable home that has just come on the market. Let's say the home sells for $115,000. You could call people whose home is in the $90,000 range and look for someone who might be in a position to make a twenty-five percent upward move.

Your call might go like this:

> M/M _____, I'm calling to let you know that we have just brought a fantastic home on the market. It's $115,000, has four bedrooms, and a beautiful view of the mountains.

Or, let's say you're in the seminars business. You might just have added a bit of material to a given seminar. Your call might go like this:

> M/M _____, I'm calling to let you know that we have just added some material on gorilla hunting to our Basic Cold Calling Seminar.

Now, we've added an element here which we hope will excite some curiosity. My prospect has got to wonder, What is a gorilla? And why do I want to hunt one in the first place?

THE CURIOSITY APPROACH

We use this approach a lot in the securities industry in helping account executives hunt for gorillas. As I mentioned earlier, a gorilla is a prospect who can cut a check for $50,000 or at least raise it in a few days' time.

Gorillas generally are not motivated as much by greed as people with less money. So to motivate a gorilla, you appeal to some motivation other than greed. One of the most powerful motivations is curiosity.

A typical reason for the call on a gorilla hunt, using the curiosity approach, might go as follows:

> M/M _____, I'm looking for a very unusual investor this evening. This investor could raise $100,000 for an exceptional opportunity.

MONEY SAVINGS

One of the oldest, and most effective, reasons for the call is an ability to save the prospect money. Regrettably, some organizations inflate a price and then offer a discount, and after a while no one believes them. And that, of course, makes it rougher going for the rest of us.

Nevertheless, it is certainly the case that a legitimate opportunity to save someone some money is a highly effective reason to call.

Here's an example from a script I wrote for a commercial real estate firm in Los Angeles:

> If I could show you a first-class building at substantially less than market, would you consider a move when your lease expires?

MORE FOR THE MONEY

Perhaps you don't want to have your prospects spend less money, but you can offer them more product for what they do spend.

Here is an example of an approach I wrote for an insurance company to go after their competitors' whole life coverage.

> M/M _____, if I could show you how to get two or three times as much insurance coverage for the money you are now spending, is this something you might want to hear about?

SCARCITY

This is one of the most powerful motivations you can play with. Even if someone is not seriously considering buying something, they'll go on and grab it anyway just to make sure that it doesn't run out. Scarcity, of course, is also very powerful to use on a close.

Here's how you might do it if you were a commercial real estate agent leasing up an office building.

> M/M _____, we've got only four prime retail spaces available in the Beam of Light Mall.

Some companies build scarcity into their entire marketing approach. A health club, for example, will have so many memberships available at a certain price. Then the price goes up. Then it only has so many of those, and so forth.

A phone call around that idea might go:

M/M _____, we only have thirty more places available at our introductory membership price. When they're gone, the price will go up five hundred dollars.

OFFER "HOW TO'S"

This method is especially important if you are selling a service. For whatever reason, people seem to like "how to's." Look at almost any self-help book jacket, and you'll see that the author will tell you that it will show you *how to* get into a cold shower, *how to* stay there, *how to* get out of it with style, *how to* dry off quickly, *how to* get into your clothes, and *how to* look radiant and healthy.

Here's an example that you could use if you were selling my seminar:

M/M _____, I'm calling to let you know that our seminar will show your sales people *how to* find more business by phone.

I am sure that there are dozens more reasons that can be used for any one product or service. But these seven certainly should spark your imagination.

Assignment: Take each type of reason for the call and write several examples of each as it might apply to your product or service.

I trust you see that in each of these reasons there is a benefit. You don't call to offer yourself a benefit. You call to offer your prospect some reason to be interested enough to listen to you.

3) The Leading Question.

Immediately following giving your reason for the call, ask a leading question. I call it a leading question because it *leads* right into a short series of qualification questions. Its primary purpose is to test interest level.

Don't make this leading question too strong. If it sounds like a closing question, people will back off because a positive answer to it implies they've bought. It's therefore important to use words that don't grab for massive amounts of commitment. Sales is, of course, a seduction, not an assault.

Some examples of good leading questions are:

- Is this the kind of thing you might want to find out more about?
- Would you be interested in hearing more about this?

As I've mentioned, never ask directly, "Are you interested?" It sounds too much like a closing question.

Here is a complete call I might design for Lee Iacocca. If I were a car salesman, every time I sold a car, I might just call everyone who lives on the same block as my new customer. Here goes my reason for the call and leading question:

> Mr. Jones, you may have seen the brand new Chrysler the Jacksons who live down the street from you just bought. It's the one that looks so good I'm sure they'll want to lock it up at night. Tell me, did you hear him lay a trail of rubber when he took off for work this morning? (Apologies to Mr. Iacocca.)

4) Interest Building/Qualification Questions

Your questions in this section follow the same rules as the questionnaire you developed for your Second Call Appointment Script. You can ask anywhere from three to ten questions in order to verify that the prospect is or is not worth seeing. One question should determine ability to make a decision. Another should check on how much money is available. And finally, you should obviously find out if the funds are available now!

Let's say you sell office furniture. Here are three key questions.

- "Fred, if you like our line, who else would be involved before a final decision is made?"
- "And how much, roughly, did you have budgeted for a redecoration?"
- "Are those funds available now?"

As you develop or refine your questions, keep in mind that the questionnaire accomplishes two goals:

1) It lets you know whether the prospect is worth pursuing.
2) Equally, if not more importantly, it provides the prospect with a way to evaluate you. The interest you show, through your questions, will be measured, and if genuine, returned.

5) The Close

Here we use the ABC closing technique, which I have already discussed.

6) After the Close

The technique is the same as previously discussed.

FIRST CALL APPOINTMENT SCRIPTS

Here's a script we use to set an appointment for one of my seminar presenters. When any one of my employees has any spare time in a city, I try to get him or her in front of a group. The script goes like this:

INTRO: Good morning/afternoon. This is _____ with Telephone Marketing. You know who we are, don't you?

IF NO: Bill Good's cold-calling seminars. Does that ring a bell?

REASON FOR CALL: How would you like a free mini-seminar on cold calling, something to pep up your brokers and get them back on the phone?

QUESTIONS:

Just a couple of quick questions.
1) How many brokers in your office?
2) How many have been with you two years or less?
3) Of the remainder, how many would you say should be doing some cold calling and aren't?

ABC CLOSE: Here's the plan. (NAME), the senior field trainer for Telephone Marketing, will be in (CITY) on (DATE). He has some free time in the morning. I would like to arrange for him to spend about an hour with your brokers. He'll give them some information they can use right then and there, and there is no cost or obligation. The only times (NAME) has available are (TIME) and (TIME). Which of those would be better for you?

AFTER THE CLOSE:

1) For this to be worthwhile for us both, we will need about an hour. Your RR's (registered representatives) will need to be on time and have an understanding with the receptionist to hold their calls. Any problems so far?

2) Let me ask you this. If you did like what (NAME) says at your free mini-seminar, and if your RR's like it too, do you have funds available now to buy the full seminar? (HE OR SHE WILL ASK PRICE). The price of the seminar is $_____ plus expenses which normally run about $_____. Would that amount pose a problem to you at this particular time?

3) Let me check your address. I have you down at _____. Is that correct?

4) Ask clarifying directions as necessary.

5) IF FREE SEMINAR IS SCHEDULED A WEEK OR MORE OFF. I will get a letter out to you right away. I will enclose a flyer that you can pass out to your brokers. The more you have attending, the more cold calling you'll get as an immediate result, okay?

6) Would you make a note in your calendar that (NAME) will be there about fifteen minutes early to visit with you and will start promptly at (TIME).

7) I'll give you a call on (DAY) just to confirm, okay?

Comment: Sometimes, I'll bury a very important question in "After the Close." I'll do that especially when I am almost certain that I'll get the answer I want. This is the case with my "Money" question in this script. Also, as you can imagine by studying the "After the Close" section of this script, we had some trouble with earlier versions. The seminar wouldn't start on time and that would throw off the entire schedule. We have pretty much eliminated that problem with this "After the Close" script and with a confirmation letter that stresses timeliness.

Carpet Cleaning Script

INTRO: May I speak with Mrs. _____, please? (RESPONSE) M/M _____, this is _____. I am with _____ Dry Carpet Cleaning. Does the name _____ Dry Carpet Cleaning ring a bell?

IF NO: We're the people who don't soak your carpets with water when we clean them.

REASON FOR CALL: Since you have just put your home on the market, I'm sure you want it to look its very best. We can help you get your home looking absolutely wonderful with our dry, professional carpet cleaning. Have you considered how clean carpets might help you sell your home?

ABC CLOSE: Here is what I suggest. I would like to drop by, measure your home, and show you how our method will make your carpets look fantastic. I will also tell you how much it would cost if you decided to let us clean them. Suppose I drop by on (DAY) at (TIME). How does that sound?

AFTER THE CLOSE:
1) I have your address as _____. Is that correct?
2) What is the nearest major cross street?
3) Do you have a pencil handy? My name again is _____. My phone number is _____. If there is any problem with (TIME) next (DAY), you'll give me a call, won't you?
4) Very good. I'll see you next (DAY), and you have a nice day, okay?

Comment: This approach quite obviously requires the list of people who have just put their homes on the market. A friendly realtor would provide such a list. Or you could call "For Sale by Owner" ads out of the classified section of the newspaper.

Gorilla Script

INTRO: May I speak with M/M _____, please? Very good. M/M _____, this is _____ with (COMPANY), members of the New York Stock Exchange. You know who we are, don't you?

IF NO: Stocks, bonds, Wall Street. Does that ring a bell?

REASON FOR CALL: M/M _____, I am looking for an unusual investor this evening. This investor could raise $50,000 for an exceptional opportunity. Am I talking with the right person or should we part company at this point?

ABC CLOSE: Very good. The investment I have in mind has returned _____% over the past _____ years. Since you are not the kind of investor who is shocked by the idea of a $50,000 investment, I also know you are the type of investor who wants to see all the facts, figures, and arithmetic before you make up your mind. Tell me, when are you most likely to have some free time during the day? (RESPONSE) I have a spot open on (DAY) at (TIME). I am also free on (DAY) at (TIME). Would you prefer to come to our office or would you prefer I come to see you?

WHAT KIND OF INVESTMENT IS IT? That's exactly what I want to show you. If the idea of $50,000 doesn't blow you away, I know you are the kind of investor who wants to see all the information, and frankly, I can't do it justice over the phone. I tell you what. If I stay longer than 15 minutes it's because you have some questions. Fair enough?

Comment: I broke some more rules on this one. My questionnaire, such as it is, is imbedded in my "Reason for Call" and my "Close." In the close, you really have to look carefully for the ABC steps, as they are all mixed up. But they're there. Also, I have written in a response to the most common question this script elicits: What kind of investment is it? I am not going to tell the prospect because most of these investments do require a detailed explanation. You might, with some justification, ask: Haven't you just violated every principle you set down about no-mystery leads? No. It's not a mystery lead. The prospect knows I am coming there to talk investment. A stiff one. I am using the fact that gorillas are a curious bunch to keep the door open and to keep the interest level up until I arrive.

FIRST CALL APPOINTMENT SCRIPT DEVELOPMENT FORM

INTRO: May I speak with M/M _____, please? Very good. M/M _____, this is _____ with (COMPANY). You know who we are, don't you?

103

REASON FOR CALL: I'm calling because _____

Tell me, _____

_____

_____ ?

QUESTIONNAIRE:

_____

_____

_____

_____

_____

_____

_____

ABC CLOSE: M/M _____, I suggest we (ACTION) _____

I can (BENEFIT) _____

I have a spot open in my calendar on (DAY) at (TIME). I am also free on (DAY) at (TIME). Which of those would be better for you?

AFTER THE CLOSE:
1) I have your address as _____, is that correct?
2) What is the nearest major cross street?
3) Do you have a pencil handy? My name again is _____. My phone number is _____. If there is any problem with _____ next (DAY), you'll give me a call, won't you?
4) Very good. I'll see you next (DAY), and you have a nice day, okay?

Assignment: Using your script rewriting skills, rewrite a first call appointment script.

6

List Development—Part I: Filling the Bathtub

If you're on track, you should have prepared a first call script and grabbed the first list you could find and made some calls. The list you grabbed might have been a good one. Most likely it wasn't a good enough list. So in the next two chapters, I'll try and help you improve your results by improving your lists. Then we'll cover how to organize and manage your lists.

Your lists are to you what a claim is to a gold prospector. It's where you find gold or not, succeed or not. Yet most salespeople don't spend one percent of their time developing their lists. Too bad.

In at least one way, the subject of list development can be compared to trying to take a bath in a tub with no plug. To take the bath, you've got to run water into the tub in spite of the fact that it's running out while you're trying to fill it. When you start stocking up on lists, you are faced with the same problem. Some of the lists you get will be no good. You have to get rid of them. Plus, you'll use them up all the time. In order to keep your "list tub" full, your first need, obviously, is to fill it. This will require you to get several hundred names or enough to call for a minimum period of six weeks without having to recycle your list. (If, for example, you are a stockbroker prospecting seven hours a week, you should be contacting about thirty people an hour or 210 per week. In six weeks, you would have contacted 1260 people. To give yourself a bit more margin, consider 1500 names to be a full bathtub.) Once you get your bathtub full, you need to keep it full by continually adding new names.

We're going to break the process of list development into two parts:

1) Filling the tub. Here we'll talk about getting names quickly;

2) Keeping it full by continually adding new names, which I'll address in Chapter 7.

Regrettably, too many salespeople are not willing to do the kind of work necessary to develop good lists. This brings to mind the classic story of two brothers who went up to their room and found it filled with horse manure. One burst into tears. The other started digging. The crybaby exclaimed, "What's wrong with you. Why are you digging?" The other brother said, "With all this crap, there's got to be a pony somewhere."

The process of list development I'm going to describe can, from one point of view, be compared to digging through a pile of manure looking for the pony. The work may be boring and certainly no fun. But there is a pony in there. If you do the work, you'll find it.

PURPOSE OF LIST DEVELOPMENT

Every once in a while I have run into the old "truth," undoubtedly held over from the Old School, that "it doesn't matter who you call, it's how many you call."

This is false. Not only does it matter who you call, but who you call can make a tremendous, indeed unbelievable, difference in your overall results.

For example, I just returned from a trip to Canada where I gave some prospecting seminars to some mutual fund salespeople. We always put everyone on the phone for the last two hours of our seminar. At the end of the phone session, one of the brokers asked me if I would get on the phone and make some calls.

"Sure," I said. "Give me a list."

Someone gave me a list from a street address directory. (For those who may not know, a street address directory is a phone book where the names and numbers are listed in street address order. Some directories will grade the streets A, B, C, D, and so on, for income range of families living on given streets; some don't do this. To find the name of the street address directory for your area, go to the local library.)

I made about four calls and said, "How much do the people on this street make?"

Someone replied, "About twenty thousand a year."

I said, "No good. Get me another street."

Someone else gave me the street he had been calling. I made four or five calls and said, "What do these houses look like?"

"Two- and three-bedroom bungalows," someone said.

"Would someone give me a street," I said, "where people make at least forty thousand a year?"

Someone found a street list with a building of $200,000 condominiums on it. On my second call, BINGO! The man I spoke with was very interested in a particular mutual fund. And he said the ten-thousand-dollar price tag would not be a problem.

Granted, some such lists would already have been prospected to death. Some won't. That's why you have to switch lists quickly if your list is loaded with pits. Who cares why they're pits? They could be pits because they don't qualify or because they aren't interested because they just received forty-two phone calls from the competition.

To find this cherry, I switched lists twice.

I could undoubtedly have found a cherry or two on these less luxurious streets. People of all incomes do save money. But there just wouldn't be enough cherries to make the search worthwhile.

With this in mind, I use list development much the way a gold miner would use a device to concentrate his or her ore. Let's say you send off a sample of ore to the assay office and find that it could produce two ounces of gold per ton of ore. If you could get rid of half a ton of dirt and lose none of the gold in the process, you would be dealing with a sample of ore that had four ounces per ton.

In sales prospecting, creative list development serves a very important function. It will concentrate your cherries, put more of them onto a single list so you don't have to make as many calls to find a good prospect. Or, to look at it another way, it will help you screen out the pits in advance. This enables you to use your non-optimum calling time to develop lists and your optimum times to make your calls. After all, there is no virtue in calling pits. Why not eliminate them through list development if you can?

THE BASIC LAWS OF LISTS

After the first year of the California Gold Rush, the "easy" claims were already taken. It's the same with lists. In any highly competitive field, the easy lists have been clobbered by every new generation of salespeople that comes along. There is a point, after all, where repetition fades into harassment, and someone receiving several calls a day has long since passed that point. Attorneys, doctors, and other obvious categories from the Yellow Pages are cases in point.

So this brings us to the two basic laws of lists.

1) The easier a list is to get, the more salespeople have it, and the less likely it is to be any good.

2) The harder a list is to get, the fewer salespeople have it, and the more profitable it's likely to be.

These laws explain why some salespeople ALWAYS find more cherries than others. They have put in the time and imagination to get better lists.

This I can tell you for sure: Your best lists will be developed by you as a result of your effort and creative thought. They won't be given to you by your sales manager, nor will you be able to buy them. This is not to say that buying lists is not important. It can be, depending on your market. But your very best ones will be developed by you.

WHAT IS A GOOD LIST?

Let's define a *Good* list (named after me, of course) as follows:

A *Good* list is any list of names, addresses, and phone numbers that has been selected according to one or more characteristics the individuals on the list have in common and that produces better results than names taken from any major free source of information.

To evaluate "goodness," you need to compare it to something. So to justify the time and expense of developing a list, we need to know that it is better than something available for free.

Let me give you an example of "one or more characteristics held in common." If you define a list according to "occupation," the individuals have one characteristic in common. For example, we could get a list of lawyers. When we specify "lawyers in New York City" we have added still another characteristic in common. Suppose we say "female lawyers in New York City under age thirty-five." We now have four characteristics in common.

And as a matter of fact, this is a list that one stockbroker used. She was a former attorney who understood attorneys, and she built up a fantastic clientele dealing only with people like herself whom she understood, liked, and could relate to. As you develop your concept of a *Good* list, you may also want to include the characteristic "someone I could like."

The more characteristics the prospects on your list have in common, the more likely you are to develop a presentation that will fit a relatively large percentage of them. Hence—more cherries per hour.

Go back to read the definition of a *Good* list again. This time, underline the following phrases:

> "One or more characteristics the individuals on the list have in common," and "major free source of information."

Let's take the flip side of the female attorney list. Let's say that you think attorneys are lower life forms along the order of guppies or paramecia. To you, spending time with an attorney is like an extra session of dental drilling. You would then, of course, take great care to exclude attorneys from your list. What's the point in coming to work in the morning if you are going to have to deal with people you don't like? I can't tell you how many salespeople I know who live half their lives in fear that some jerk they regrettably sold something to will call. Why even sell to them in the first place? If there are certain types of people you don't like, try your best to exclude them from your list. Failing that, don't sell to them.

If it's not fun, don't do it!

How Good is *Good?*

The definition of a *Good* list we have been considering so far doesn't give you any idea of how good is good. So let's expand our definition:

> A *Good* list is any list that will generate a minimum of three cherries per hour.

I have been able to get three cherries per hour in virtually every industry I have worked in. And this ranges from securities to insurance to residential real estate to commercial real estate to high tech and to long distance communications firms.

To achieve three or more cherries per hour, I keep working with the list, the message, and time of day I call until I can produce at least three cherries an hour. If you tell me you are getting three cherries an hour, I'm certain you've got a campaign you can take to the bank.

There is no question that some lists can be considered good at two cherries an hour, one an hour, or even one every several hours. The exceptions to the three-an-hour rule will depend in part upon the price of the goods or service you're selling.

If you are selling an office building worth forty million dollars, you would have to have one mighty good list to get three people per hour interested in it. However, by researching real estate buyers for major insurance companies, private syndicates, and major public partnerships, you might well be able to come up with one.

If you are an insurance agent looking for pension fund money, one cherry every couple of hours might be the best you can do. This is an extremely competitive market, and some pension fund managers will get literally dozens of calls a day from insurance agents and stockbrokers.

If you can't conceivably come up with three cherries per hour, then for you, a *Good* list would be defined according to however many cherries you, or the best prospector in your firm, can produce per hour *with your best efforts.*

I should also add that I am assuming fifty to sixty dials of the phone an hour. If you're doing twelve calls an hour and not getting three cherries an hour, don't blame me. Push up your numbers and then see what you can get. (See Chapter 10.)

LIST SELECTION PRINCIPLES

In the remainder of this chapter, I'll go over with you the first of two principles of list development we'll be using. Since there are so many applications for telemarketing, it would be impossible to give detailed sources for each industry.

So my objective in the remainder of this chapter is to help you learn to "think lists." Once you know how to think about the subject, simply take your body down to the local public library, tell the librarian what you are looking for, and start from there.

If you don't have access to a decent library, you'll just have to go to a city where there is one. If you can find yourself a good library, I promise you not just a leg up on the competition, but several other body parts as well.

THE LOOK-ALIKE PRINCIPLE

The first principle we'll explore is the "look-alike" principle. It states:

- **Your best prospect is someone who already buys your product or service or who looks like someone who already buys your product or service.**

Read it again. This time underline the phrases "already buys" and "looks like."

This is a simple principle. Here is how it works. Suppose you are a Cadillac salesman. If you could go down to the Department of Motor Vehicles (which you can in a lot of states) and copy down the names and addresses of Cadillac owners, you've got a list of people who are statistically most likely to buy what you sell. (You could also check with a list broker and buy such a list.)

Obviously, for some of you, your best prospect list contains people who already buy what you sell *from you.* I'm really not going to be talking about getting more business from your present customers. I'm much more interested in helping you get new customers, so let's talk about people *who look like* people you already do business with.

Where could you get people who look like Cadillac owners?

I would call up Cadillac owners and ask them some questions, for example:

1) How old are you?

2) What kind of car did you drive before you bought a Cadillac?

3) How old were you when you bought your first Cadillac?

4) How many in your family?

5) What magazines do you subscribe to?

6) How much money do you make?

7) What do you do for a living?

From these questions alone, I could begin putting together some ideas of where to get a list of look-alikes. One thing I would do is call a list broker (listed in the Yellow Pages under Mailing List Brokers) and order a list of people who own Lincolns (or whatever kind of car people own before they buy Cadillacs), who are in a certain age bracket, and who subscribe to whatever magazines were mentioned most frequently.

How many Cadillac owners do you need to call to come up with some look-alike list ideas? Somewhere between one and one hundred. I am definitely not recommending you do any kind of scientific survey. All you are looking for is a source of ideas to develop your prospecting list. The real "scientific" test comes when you try out your list to see if it will yield three cherries per hour or whatever you find to be a profitable result. All I want you to do is call up some Cadillac owners to get an idea of *where to look to find people likely to buy Cadillacs.*

Here is how your call might go:

YOU: Mr. Jones, this is Joe Dokes here at the ABC Cadillac
          Dealers. Do you have just a moment?

JONES: Sure, what can I do for you?

YOU: First of all, I'm not calling to sell you anything. I'm just
          doing an informal survey of current Cadillac owners.
          Your answers to my questions will simply help me do
          a better job finding new customers. On that basis, may
          I run some questions by you?

Most people will be extremely willing to help. That has certainly
been my experience.

Let me give you an example of how I used this look-alike
principle in researching and developing a new seminar.

In 1985 I developed and brought on line a seminar for residential real estate agents. In the residential real estate business, the
agents' primary objective is to find people who want to sell a
house. If a real estate agent has no property to sell, he or she has
nothing to show and nothing to sell.

In a very real sense, everyone who owns a home is a prospect
for a real estate agent. After all, very few people stay in the same
house their entire lives. Traditional prospecting in real estate is
based around this fact. It's called "farming," and each real estate
agent is assigned a "farm" of 250 to 500 homes. He or she is
expected to contact everyone in that farm and establish a reputation as the person most knowledgeable about real estate in that
area. Over time, as the agent becomes known, people who decide
to sell will call that agent and give him or her the listing.

There are several problems with this method in today's market.
First, most homeowners today are two-income families. This
means that the only time available for contacting the homeowners
is at night or on the weekend. Since farming is traditionally done
door-to-door, this creates a big problem. In today's troubled
times, who wants to take a chance walking door-to-door at night?
And weekends are the very best time to show houses to buyers.
So this leaves no time for developing listings, and with no houses

to sell, you've got nothing to advertise, no signs on property to attract potential buyers, and no commission.

Farming does work. There are many real estate agents driving Cadillacs and living the good life because of it. But it takes a lot of time. Most people I know in real estate estimate it will take six to eighteen months for a farm to begin producing a steady stream of new sellers. You could starve to death in the meantime.

My objective in researching the residential real estate market was to develop a method that would work *faster* than farming. So I took a fresh look at the problem of real estate prospecting.

My theory was that while everyone who owns a house *is* a prospect, there have to be ways to develop lists of people who are *statistically more likely to sell* than the average homeowner.

So in my research, I simply applied the look-alike principle and called up one hundred people who currently had their homes listed on the market. If you want to find out what a prospective home seller looks like in order to develop profitable lists of them, talk to one hundred people who are currently trying to sell a home.

Here are some of the questions I asked:

- How long have you lived at your present address?

- Who is currently listing your home?

- How did you first make contact with your agent?

- How long before you listed did you know your agent?

- How long before you put your home on the market did you start thinking and talking about selling?

- Was there any special situation that occurred just before you made the decision to sell?

- Why are you selling?

- Did you attempt to sell your house yourself before you listed with a real estate company?

- Do you have any children? What age? Have any of them left home or graduated from high school or college recently?

- Have you bought a new car, boat, or recreational vehicle within the last year? Which and what kind?

Here are some of the results.

- Forty-three percent of the people with a home on the market have bought a new car, van, or station wagon within the past year! Now does that suggest a list to you?

- Eleven percent were going to build or were in the process of building. This, of course, suggests that a list of lot owners would be a wonderful list of potential listers.

- Eleven percent said their house was too small. I asked myself the obvious question. Why would a house be too small? Answer: a recent addition to the family. So I dug into birth announcements in the newspapers from two years ago, looked for current phone numbers, and couldn't find many at all. Well over fifty percent had moved. So I went to the one-year-old lists. Bingo! A real estate agent calling people who had a child one year ago will average *two listing appointments an hour* on this list. Plus, you can pick up two or three prospects who are thinking about a move within the next several months. These results are almost infinitely better than a real estate agent can expect from just cold calling a random list of homeowners.

- Seven percent said their home was too large. This suggested some very interesting lists. One obvious one was parents of newly married couples. These people have homes much too large now. Plus, many parents are going to be helping their newlywed children get their first house. This list of course can be found in the marriage announcements in the paper.

I think you see the idea. You can get terrific ideas for lists by looking for people *who look just like* people you already do business with or who already buy your product, perhaps from someone else.

A warning: Many of your list ideas may be turkeys. Don't worry about that. All you need is just one *Good* one that will enable you to get three or four times the results than competing salespeople get.

I am sure you have noticed that many of the list ideas I developed for our real estate seminar came from newspapers. Most newspapers will gladly make their back copies available for your study, and many of them have rooms set aside for research. Rather than keep bulky newspaper files, many papers make available microfilm files of back issues. These are also available in most public libraries.

To give you an idea of the difference between good lists and bad lists, one of our early test clients was a Century 21 office in Salt Lake City. Before we showed them which lists to use, a two-hour phone blitz with ten agents calling produced no listing appointments. On the night of our seminar, ten people called *Good* lists for less than an hour and got eleven appointments— good, solid listing appointments with people who were genuinely interested in selling their homes. The good list made all the difference.

NO SURVEY NEEDED TO GET STARTED

Please don't wait to start list development until after you have talked to one hundred of your own customers or people who use your product. There are some obvious look-alikes you can pull together right now. And for many markets, you don't need a survey to determine who the look-alikes are. Think simply and go to the obvious sources.

Streets on Which Good Clients Live

In any of the financial services, you can develop excellent lists simply by using the list of people who live on the same street as your client. This list is available, of course, from the street address directory. If you don't have any good clients yet, get the streets on which the top salespeople from your office live. (As an interesting side note, very few good brokers or insurance agents will sell to their neighbors.) Apply the look-alike principle to help you select names from major free sources such as Yellow Pages, street address directories, and manufacturers' guides.

Same Occupation

The ideal occupation list is one that is not represented in the Yellow Pages. I asked a broker one time who his best client was. He said, "It's a guy who designs packaging for different products."

I said, "Would you like to have more like him?"

His reply was, "Are you kidding? I've checked the Yellow Pages and there are none listed." He was certainly correct that package designers were not listed in the Yellow Pages. They tend to work for big corporations and advertising agencies, and so are not listed separately.

To get a list of package designers, we first checked a standard library book, *The Encyclopedia of Associations.* We found there was an association of package designers based in New York with some three thousand members. The broker called them and asked, "How many members do you have in Southern California?"

"Four hundred."

He then asked, "How do I get a copy of the membership directory?"

"Send me twenty-seven dollars," was the reply.

Now how many stockbrokers do you think regularly cold call the list of package designers? Not many. And that's the entire idea.

Same Activity

Let's suppose your best client is a dog enthusiast. He breeds champion greyhounds. I guarantee you that he knows every other greyhound breeder in the state. Therefore, the Greyhound Breeders Association directory is a list on which that all-important word of mouth can occur. There may not be but a handful of breeders. Or there may be a bunch. The place to start looking for the list is either in the Yellow Pages under Kennel Clubs or in the *Directory of Directories,* which is also found in any decent public library. Or check the *Encyclopedia of Associations.* First go to the key-word index and look up "kennel," "greyhound," or even "dog." The key word index will list the names of directories dealing with these subjects and how to get them. (A note on Kennel Club directories: Some of them will indicate which of their members employ an agent to show their dogs for them. For this they pay a lively $15,000 a year minimum. So if you are looking for a look-alike list that also has M O N E Y, rest assured that people who spend at least $15,000 a year on their dogs are not down to their last dime.)

By the way, many of the directories available will contain unlisted numbers. This is excellent because people with unlisted numbers don't receive their fair share of cold calls. However, you will frequently be asked, "How did you get my number?" Try any of these three responses.

- "I got it from the Austin Kennel Club Directory" (or whichever directory you used).

- "I'm not sure. My assistant handles that. If you will hang on a few minutes I'll have him look it up." (PAUSE) (No one in the history of the world has ever volunteered to stay on hold.)

- "I got it from a list of people who are supposed to have money. Did they make a mistake?"

This third response will usually get a chuckle and any resistance to your call will lesson with the laugh. Laughter is, after all, terrific medicine, for colds as well as cold calling.

If someone insists on knowing where you got their name, tell 'em.

Purchased Lists

Certainly one way to get lists is to rent them. I say "rent" as opposed to "buy" because very literally you rent them for a one-time use. List brokers typically "seed the list" with dummy names. Every time you mail to the list, at least one or two letters go back to the list broker. If you paid for this list once and mail to it twice, expect a nasty note from the list broker's attorney ordering you to pay up.

However, once you have contacted someone by phone, for all intents and purposes, it's *your name*.

Here are some recommendations on how to select a list broker:

1) Check the Yellow Pages under Mailing List Brokers. If the choices seem limited or poor, go to the library and check the Manhattan Yellow Pages. As with advertising, publishing, and a host of other communication activities, New York City is the list brokerage capital.

2) Try and find someone who has dealt with markets such as yours. Ask for references.

3) Let the list broker earn his or her commission. (Commission is generally built into the price.) Instead of telling the list broker what

list you want to buy, describe the kind of customer you want, and let the broker make some recommendations. He or she may well know the market better than you.

4) On an initial order, don't order more than one thousand names. Many list brokers will require a minimum order of five thousand. An individual certainly doesn't need five thousand names.

5) Ask what percentage of the list is guaranteed accurate, meaning correct name and address. Eighty percent accurate is your very bottom requirement.

6) Check to see if the list comes with phone numbers, but don't necessarily eliminate a list if they are not available. Hire someone to look up the numbers and the chances are that you will have a list of prospects who have not been called.

7) As with anything you buy, you generally get what you pay for. On a very low end, I have seen lists for $35 per thousand. On a high end, they can run $250 per thousand. The average price for decent lists can run $85–$125 per thousand names. Generally, the more specialized the list, the more expensive it is.

8) Don't hang onto a bum list. After several tests, if you can't get a profitable response from the list, throw it out. Better yet, stuff it in a company envelope, write "HOT PROSPECTS—$100,000 MINI-MUM" on it, and leave it in the elevator where your biggest competitor works. Then continue your search for a *Good* list.

To get an idea of the staggering number of direct mail lists available, go to the library and spend a few hours with a two-volume set of books called *Standard Rate and Data: Direct Mail Lists.* This is the list of commercially available lists.

HOW MANY NAMES DO YOU NEED?

This is a tough question, and the answer will vary tremendously by industry and by quality of list. You don't need an infinite number of names. When you get a good list, you'll keep it and call it again in forty-five to ninety days depending on your industry and product. So how many do you need? Here are some rules of thumb.

1) If you are in financial services, you need about three thousand names *if you are new in the business.* Of these three thousand, you

119

need approximately two thousand names to call during the day and one thousand for nighttime calling. If you have been around a year or longer and have built up a customer base, you can start with fifteen hundred names. Of these, one thousand should be for daytime calling and five hundred for nighttime.

2) In real estate, you need maybe fifty names a week developed in the manner I discussed to generate five good listing appointments a week.

3) In other industries, you'll need to do some arithmetic to figure out how many names you need. First, figure out how many *contacts* it takes for you to achieve your weekly objective. Let's say you are a Cadillac salesperson and that you want to see 10 new people in the showroom each week. Let's further assume that to get 10 people in the showroom, you need to set 15 appointments to allow for no-shows. To set one appointment you need to contact 25 people on your look-alike list. So to set 15 appointments, you need to contact 375 (15 $\times$ 25) people each week.

Second, multiply your weekly needs by 8. So in this case, you will need a "bathtub" of 3000 names (8 $\times$ 375). This gives you enough names to last 8 weeks. Then, if you are getting your 10 people in the shop each week, and if that is profitable to you, start at the beginning of the list.

THINK LIKE A FISHERMAN

There is a certain way you need to think in order to find good lists. I call this mode of thought "fisherperson think." Let me give you an example.

Suppose you are going fishing one morning, but your alarm doesn't go off, and you get off to a late start. As you walk down to the lake, you see an old codger with a string of fish thrown over his shoulder. Naturally, you have some questions.

YOU: Where did you catch 'em?

CODGER: Down at the lake.

Now, if you are not much of a fisherperson, you would let it go at that and wander on down to the lake. But if you are a real fisherperson, you would continue the conversation.

120

YOU: Where down at the lake?

CODGER: By the big rock.

YOU: You mean the one over by the willow tree?

CODGER: Yep.

YOU: What were you using for bait?

CODGER: Plastic worm.

YOU: Great. Thanks.

Take a look at your present clients as if they were that string of fish hanging down from the codger's back. What pond did they come from? Or to put it in sales prospecting terms, "What list could they have come from?"

You are looking for lists of people *on which your client appears.* Ideally, there will be a connection between the people on the list which will make *word of mouth possible.* Given a choice between a list of people who own a Mercedes-Benz and a Mercedes Owners Club directory, *always* take the list on which word of mouth can occur. Get the club directory.

LIST DEVELOPMENT ASSIGNMENT

1) Sit down with your present account book or customer list. (If you don't already have clients, get your manager to spend some time with you and let you study other salespeople's clients.)

2) Open it to your best customer.

3) Write down what you know about him or her, in business, and where appropriate, personally.

4) Ask yourself, where can I get a list of people *most like my client* and on which he or she appears?

5) Continue your look-alike analysis (include a survey if necessary) until you have five good list ideas.

6) Get the lists.

7

List Development—Part II: How to Keep the Bathtub Full

Let's go back to our comparison of list development with taking a bath in a tub with no plug.

Using the principles in Chapter 6, first fill the tub with look-alike lists. If you need fifteen hundred names, you'll no doubt go through a lot more than that to find those lists that will get you three cherries or better an hour or whatever optimum number you've established for your particular product or service. These lists will then become the "limited market" that you are going to try and dominate.

But even when you have assembled your target market, your lists will immediately start to shrink, because as you begin calling you'll remove the cherries. When you find a cherry, you'll simply scratch the name off the list and start a 4 × 6 card. (We'll come to call-back files and how to manage your prospect cards in Chapter 8.) Scratch off your green cherries and start 4 × 6 cards on them too. Naturally you'll remove disconnected numbers from your list, and, of course, jerks. A heavy prospecting campaign can remove as many as fifty to seventy-five names per week. Be careful not to cycle through your list several times without replacing any names or your list will get so small you'll be recycling it too often. And, as I mentioned earlier, repetition can fade into harassment.

The solution is simple. Keep the list at fifteen hundred names by adding a name for each you remove. I'll use the term "replacement list" to refer to the sources of names that will replace the names you have used up.

If you truly hate to cold call, you will pay very close attention now to the three major sources of replacement names I will cover.

They are:

1) Change lists

2) Referral lists

3) Connections lists

While I will be discussing these principles primarily as a source of replacement names—fresh water for your bathtub—some of you, notably real estate agents, should consider only lists from these sources. As a rule, they are so much better than other available lists, it's a shame not to spend the time to start off with the best. A little time put in on developing lists from these sources means a lot fewer cold calls to achieve a given result.

A note of warning: It can be very time-consuming to develop replacement names in the manner I'll be discussing. You will have to decide for yourself whether you want to spend this kind of time. The trade-off is that the better the list, the fewer hours you have to spend to achieve a given result. Look at it this way: If you could develop a list of absolutely fantastic prospects, you wouldn't have to call very much, now would you? These principles of list development I am going to discuss with you are so powerful, that if you only follow them to replace names coming off your list, you will upgrade your list tremendously over time. If you were to develop an entire list using these principles, you would be a formidable competitor.

THE CHANGE PRINCIPLE OF LIST REPLACEMENT AND DEVELOPMENT

Let me first state the change principle of list development. Then I will give an example of it and discuss its application to various markets. The change principle can be stated as a variation of Newton's law of motion as follows:

- **Others things being equal, a person or company in process of change finds additional change easier to make. Therefore, if you are able to extract names of people in process of change from a given list, the change list will produce better**

123

results than the list from which the change names were originally drawn.

Newton, of course, said it this way:

"A body in motion tends to remain in motion, a body at rest to remain at rest, unless acted on by an outside force."

To show you how the change principle might apply, consider this example.

Suppose you are a stockbroker. You call a person this evening who is forty-two years old. He has been working at the same bank since receiving his MBA from the University of Chicago seventeen years ago. He is now an executive vice-president earning $65,000 a year. He has been married to the same woman for eighteen years. Their oldest child is seventeen years old and a senior in high school, and the youngest is fifteen and a sophomore. They live in a four-bedroom home, and he has driven the same route to work for the past eight years. Their three children have all gone to the same school system. Every Saturday night they play cards with the Stones, and for three weeks every summer they go to the same beach house. He has the same broker he has had for the past twelve years.

As you imagine phoning up this person tonight, ask yourself this question: Based on what you know about him and his lifestyle, how likely is he to change the way he invests his money? Not very likely, right? He's in a period where his life is stable, and surely he doesn't want to upset any apple carts.

Now, let's age him ten years. He is fifty-two. Five months ago, he was made the senior vice-president at the bank. He earns $145,000 a year. All of the children are now out of college, and he and his wife have recently sold the four-bedroom house and bought a luxury condominium. She sold the station wagon and bought a Mercedes, and he sold the Oldsmobile and now drives a Porsche. Instead of going to the beach house, they now take a three-week trip to some exotic place in the world. They have had the same broker now for twenty-two years. They just completed the redecoration of the new condo three weeks ago.

Let's ask the same question we asked about him ten years earlier. How likely do you think he is to change the way he invests his money when you phone him up tonight? Is he more likely to be open to a change than he was in the previous example?

My answer is an unequivocal YES. He will definitely be more open because other things are changing in his life as well. One more change won't upset the apple cart because *it is already upset!* It therefore doesn't make any difference if he changes still something else. And chances are he is tired of the same old broker anyway.

Here is another example. Suppose you have a list of five hundred homeowners and you want to know which are likely prospects to sell their home in the next year. To find out, you can call each and every one and ask. Or, if you are lazy, you can develop lists of homeowners *in the process of change.* I can state without question that in real estate, change lists are five to ten times better than geographic lists of homeowners.

To summarize: our objective, then, is to extract certain names from our basic look-alike lists that are better than the lists from which they are drawn.

A couple of points of clarification:

- First, your change lists do not literally need to be drawn from the exact look-alike lists you developed earlier. Homeowners who had filed for divorce would still look just like other homeowners on your list except for the one fact of change. And I can promise you: homeowners who have filed for divorce are a better set of names for selling a house than homeowners at random.

- Second, you might wonder, why not use only these lists? Quite obviously, you won't need as many names because of the much higher concentration of cherries. If you are willing to spend quite a few hours putting together, say, five hundred to one thousand names, go for it! Realistically, however, most salespeople need a quick start, and sales managers are leery of salespeople who run off and start organizing. That's why I recommend you start with look-alike lists and use the change principle as the source of your replacement names.

With these points of clarification in mind, let's talk about the application of the change principle in three broad markets: corporate, individual daytime, and individual nighttime. By corporate, I mean those markets where you are selling to businesses. By

125

daytime, I mean those products and services you sell to individuals you can contact during the day. And by nighttime, I mean those markets you approach by calling people at home. Some products that can be sold at night can also be sold during the day, of course, and vice versa.

Change in the Corporate Market

The change principle is easy to visualize if you are accustomed to prospecting the corporate market. In many corporations, when someone new gets appointed to a position, he or she often sweeps out any remnants of the old regime. This holds great promise if you are on the outside trying to get in. If you are on the inside, when the shake-up comes, you can find yourself swept away if you don't take quick action when the sweep starts.

As you search for corporate change, look for *any* change. When a corporation is in the middle of an expansion, a new product introduction, a reorganization, or a buy-out, the same principles apply: Change is easier when it is happening from some other cause.

Your best sources of corporate change are internal corporate newspapers and trade papers. Virtually every corporation with one hundred employees or more, puts out some kind of in-house newsletter, or house organ as it's sometimes called. These are unbelievably easy to get. The easiest way to get a corporate paper is to simply ask a client to put his copy in an envelope and send it when he's done with it. Better yet, send him or her a dozen self-addressed, stamped envelopes. You can also call the editor of the house organ and ask to be put on the list to receive the paper. Some corporations make theirs available as a public relations gesture to anyone who expresses interest.

If you are really serious about pursuing internal corporate papers, you should go to the library and study a book called *Working Press of the Nation,* Volume 5. This is a source of major corporate papers and how to get them. Some may cost you a subscription fee, but I understand from speaking to senior executives in major sales organizations that salespeople are never prohibited from spending some of their own money to promote their own careers.

Another important source of change information is trade papers. A trade paper is a newspaper that goes only to a given occupation or industry. For instance, once when I was doing some research in the Los Angeles City library, which has one of the great collections of lists and librarians who know about lists, I came across a copy of a trade paper called *Southern California Retailer.* As an exercise, I decided to count promotion announcements. I gave up when I passed ninety and still had more than half the paper yet to go.

On the front cover of this particular issue was a picture headlined "New Sony Marketing Team." Sony evidently had brought in heavy management to handle the Southern California market. At a minimum the members of this team would be good prospects for a stockbroker, insurance agent, real estate agent, auto leasing, banking, furniture, clothing, credit cards, and so on, and so on.

To find out if there is a trade paper put out in the industry you are interested in, ask several people who are part of the industry. Find out if they belong to an association. Or, go to the library and spend some time with the *Encyclopedia of Associations* and look up the industry in the key word index. Call the association. Also, check the Yellow Pages under associations and see what is available locally.

If you begin to check into some of the sources I've mentioned in this section, you will discover that *the amount of information available on people in the process of corporate change is staggering.*

If for no other reason, calling new kids on the block is easier than old kids, because the new kids don't yet have their administrative defense screens in place.

The Change Principle in Individual Markets

The change principle applies not only to corporations but to individuals as well. It's just a bit less obvious.

It appears that individuals go through periods of stability and periods of change. And in these periods of change, a lot of things change, many of them *apparently* unrelated. But there is something that unites the apparently different changes, and it is simply *the fact of change.*

In many industries, insurance for instance, pieces of this principle have been grasped. For years, insurance agents have been advised to call a "new birth list." The assumption is that a new birth in the family gives rise to heightened responsibility and additional needs for protection and coverage. Frankly, I don't think "additional needs" or "added responsibility" has much to do with it at all. I think that the new birth list is good because of the fact that it represents a *change in the family,* and where there is one change, there are likely to be others.

THE CHANGE PRINCIPLE IN INDIVIDUAL DAYTIME MARKET

In many industries, especially all areas of financial services, you can prospect individuals at work. You can't spend too much time at it because there is an inherent conflict of interest in handling a matter of personal affairs on the boss's time. But it can be done, especially since my method doesn't take much of your prospect's time.

As an example, one broker I know built his entire book of business on the change principle in daytime markets. He told me that when he was getting started, he and his wife used to go around and pick up the local "shopper" newspapers in their area every Thursday. They would cut out all the promotion announcements, and then he would give those promoted a call. His approach, which I have now incorporated into a recently promoted executives script, went like this:

> Hello, Mr. Jones, this is (NAME) with (COMPANY). I am calling to congratulate you on your promotion and let you know that I have some excellent ideas to help you invest some of that new money.

His theory was that one way to grow as a broker was to get clients on the way up. He told me that several of his clients whose names he first got from local promotion announcements went on to become chief executive officers of Forbes 500 corporations.

Here are some sources of change names who can be contacted during the day. They would be prospects for almost any expensive item, whether securities, insurance, property, or automobiles.

RECENTLY PROMOTED EXECUTIVES

Generally, when a promotion is announced in a major daily newspaper, a deluge of calls follows . . . and then silence. So wait a few days or even several weeks. Then call. Better yet, scour corporate and trade papers. They're loaded, harder to get than daily newspaper promotion announcements, and therefore less likely to be hammered.

You can also purchase a recently promoted executive list. Specify to your list broker that you want to subscribe to the change-of-address notices list made available from McGraw-Hill, the publisher of *Business Week* and other trade magazines. Don't contact McGraw-Hill directly. Contact your mailing list broker. A very large percentage of these change-of-address names have changed due to a promotion. Even when a person does not change location, if he or she is promoted from second vice-president to first vice-president, they will file change-of-address notices so that not even the mail room person remembers they were ever anything but first vice-president.

BUYERS AND SELLERS OF COMMERCIAL PROPERTY

In virtually every county in the United States there is a *Journal of Record*. This is a publication that comes out anywhere from daily to quarterly and lists transactions of public record. "Public record" means that anyone is entitled to know about them. It includes liens, divorces, marriages, wills filed for probate, and sale of real property. When a piece of commercial property, income residential property, or raw land is sold, you can be certain that a substantial piece of money changed hands. The seller got some. The real estate agent got some. There is surely a lawyer in there somewhere.

You definitely want to contact the seller of the property. However, buyers are also good prospects because they have likewise gone through a major change. And don't forget the agent, broker, lawyer, and maybe the title insurer.

NEW CONSTRUCTION PROJECTS

When a person or company is expanding, redecorating, or constructing a new building, a building permit is required. There is a company (McGraw-Hill again) that investigates these building permits, breaks them down into categories, and publishes them. The reports are called *The Dodge Reports* and are available in most any public library. If you can't locate *The Dodge Reports* in your area, go and investigate the city or county department that issues building permits. It will tell you who is expanding, remodeling, and redecorating. And that will tell you who has some money.

LEGAL SETTLEMENT

Some of the best securities accounts I know of have been obtained by calling people who have just received a legal settlement. These will frequently be announced in your local *Journal of Record* or daily newspaper. They will sometimes be announced in local business papers. So if you are selling any kind of expensive item, certainly consider people who have just got a good chunk of money. One of the few times to call a lawyer is when he or she has walked away with pockets stuffed with contingency settlement money.

SALE OF BUSINESS

This information is available in the business pages of local newspapers, trade papers, and through changes in licensing at the local business license bureau.

The Change Principle in Individual Nighttime Market

If you are prospecting a residential market, there are lots of sources of change names.

PARENTS OF NEWLYWEDS

These need to be dug out of the marriage announcements of your local paper. Keep in mind that any one marriage announcement can be worth two or more sets of names. Here are people whose lifestyle is changing dramatically for the better. The bride's parents may be choking on the wedding bill. But the groom's parents may be getting ready to live it up. So let the bride's parents have a couple of months to recover and go after the groom's parents first.

PEOPLE SELLING EXPENSIVE CARS

This list is of course available in the classified section in the local newspaper. In a bright, cheerful voice, make your call as follows:

YOU: *Ring, ring.*

PROSPECT: Hello.

YOU: Is this the person with the Mercedes for sale?

PROSPECT: Yes.

YOU: Very good. I have some good news and some bad news for you. Which would you like to hear first?

PROSPECT: The good news.

YOU: Let me give you the bad news first. I am not calling for the Mercedes. The good news is I am calling to let you know that I have a fantastic place for you to put some of that money when you sell it. May I mention an idea to you?

PROSPECT: Sure, what is it?

YOU: By the way, who am I speaking with?

PROSPECT: Jack Jones.

Now you have the prospect's name and his unlisted phone number. By the way, classified ads are frequently filled with unlisted phone numbers and this is one of the few sources for them. Like other hard-to-reach people, these individuals don't get their fair share of solicitation phone calls.

131

OWNERS SELLING THEIR OWN HOME OR OTHER PROPERTIES

These prospects are also available in the classified section of the newspaper. In the real estate industry, they are known as "Fizbos" which is the pronunciation for the abbreviation for the initials FSBO, which mean "For Sale By Owner." Real estate people call Fizbos all the time, so it is not a bad idea to allow the ad to age for a week if you are going after them to sell them something other than a house.

HOMEOWNERS SELLING HOMES WITH LOTS OF EQUITY

This list can be extracted from a Multiple Listing Book for your area. This is theoretically available only to members of the real estate profession who belong to a multiple listing board. But if you're friendly with a real estate agent, you can usually get someone to give you last week's copy. The Multiple Listing Book is a record of all homes on the market that are listed with real estate agents. To get the list of homeowners with lots of equity, simply study the book and look for homeowners who have owned their home at least ten years. They will be the ones profiting from the real estate boom that began in the 1970's.

If you go after people who may have owned their home fifteen or twenty years or longer, you could be in for a major cash find. Anyone over the age of fifty-five who sells a home may take a one-time capital gains exclusion, which at this writing equals $125,000. This means that he or she does not have to pay any capital gains tax on up to $125,000 profit on sale of a primary residence. Before age fifty-five, a person selling a home with a lot of equity has to invest in another home of at least equal value. Otherwise, he or she has to pay a tax. However, where there is lots of equity, there will usually be some cash available for other things. Here's how it might work even if the individual is not over fifty-five or is not going to take the one-time exclusion.

A homeowner may have purchased a $50,000 home in 1974 and sells it for $225,000 in 1986. He purchases a new home for $245,000 but instead of putting all his $175,000 cash from the sale of his previous home into his new home, he may only put down the required twenty percent or about $50,000. As long as he has purchased a home *of equal or greater value,* he can do whatever he wants with his cash.

So if you can develop a prospect that will soon be getting his hands on a lot of money, why not?

HEIRS

Some people seem to think it is a terribly morbid idea to call the heirs of people recently deceased. My point of view is that this is a period of great and dramatic change. Estates will be restructured. Homes and property will be sold. Assets divided up. Someone will get this business. Why not you?

The obvious place to get these names is in the obituary notices in the local paper. If you want to take this one step further, you can go to the courthouse and ask to see the wills that have been filed for probate. These are all available to the public. When you read in the newspaper that a famous person has died and left four million dollars to his cat, rest assured that the enterprising reporter who wrote the story used the same public record.

In dealing with the heirs list, it is in bad taste to call too soon and refer to your source of information. You would never call someone and say, "I was rummaging around in the basement of the courthouse recently and noticed that your Aunt Matilda left you a bundle." Just deal with the person with tact and courtesy, as you would with any other person.

Tips on Developing Change Names

Copying down names at courthouses and cutting them out of newspapers does not require extraordinary amounts of skill and intelligence. In fact, it's a no-brainer. So I recommend that once you have developed your source of names and have tested it to make certain it produces worthwhile results when called, find a literate high school student and pay him or her to develop your names. If he or she gets ten names an hour, it's only costing you about thirty-three cents a name. And that's cheaper than you can buy some of the more expensive lists. It could cost you ten to fifteen dollars a week to keep your list refreshed with first-rate change names.

133

THE REFERRAL PRINCIPLE OF LIST REPLACEMENT AND DEVELOPMENT

Certainly a list of people to whom you are referred is almost your best list. I say almost, because your best list is a list of people you know. Certainly referral lists are suitable candidates to replace the names that fall off your everyday look-alike lists. Some of you reading this book right now may be able to build such a large referral list that you'll never need to cold call again.

But for some reason that is entirely unknown to me, salespeople in every industry will work hard, do a good job, develop a good rapport with a client, and not ever, not once, ask for referrals. One insurance company I ran across trains their agents to ask for "two but not more than three" referrals. Why stop at three? Why not ask for fifty or one hundred? Why stay on food stamps? Break loose! Ask for lots of referrals.

One secret to building your referral list is simply to ask everyone you talk to, whether client or prospect, for referrals. You may not get many from people you don't know well, but lots of little creeks make up the Mississippi River.

When routinely asking for referrals, don't ask: "Do you know anyone that I might call?" A better question is: "Who do you know that I might contact about _____?"

Here is a simple technique that is always good for at least two referrals if you have accounts who are individuals. Go to the street address directory and copy down the names of your clients' next-door neighbors into your account record sheet or folder. Make sure you write down the phone numbers, because if things go according to plan, you'll need them. Next time you are talking with your good customer the conversation should go like this:

> "Joe, this is Fred Smithers over here at Beam of Light. A couple of your neighbors came up on one of my market lists, but before I called them I wanted to check with you and see if it's okay with you if I mention that you are one of my good customers. Do you know John Jones and Jack Johnson?"

After you have got permission to call John Jones and Jack Jackson, then ask, "Who else do you know on _____ there that I might call about _____? What about where you work? Who there should I contact?"

If your customer will give you two referrals, you can get more. I had a salesman in Louisiana call five of his clients and ask each about ten of his neighbors. He got eleven referrals! One of his clients said, "Oh sure, give 'em a call. And by the way, Fred Blather who lives down the street just got a big promotion with the telephone company. Call him too."

After conducting this test, the salesman told me that he had tried to prove it wouldn't work by calling people he had asked for referrals within the previous thirty days. He had not got one referral by simply asking, "Do you know anyone I could call about their insurance needs?" By asking permission to call *named individuals he knew they knew*, he had picked up eleven referrals.

For those of you who would like to get a whole bunch of referrals at one time, an even better technique is to sit down with a customer and go over a *list of people that he or she is likely to know.* Here is one of many cases in which I did it.

I did a seminar a while back for one of the major insurance companies. At the end of the seminar, the general agent (GA) was very pleased. I first asked him for a copy of the GA directory for that company, which he gave me. Then I asked him to look it over —there were several hundred names in it—and check off the GA's he felt were big enough to afford one of our seminars. He took maybe ten or fifteen minutes to do this. Finally, I said, "Jack, would you mind if I contact these people and mention that you are a happy client?"

"No problem."

Bingo! I had over fifty referrals! A person could starve to death asking for "two but not more than three" referrals.

THE CONNECTION PRINCIPLE OF LIST REPLACEMENT AND DEVELOPMENT

People like doing business with people they know. As you progress with my system, you'll come to understand that it is *designed* to introduce you to lots of people and give you the opportunity to get to know them.

But what if you already know lots of people? Why not use them? Many, if not most, salespeople not only do not, but will not, use their connections. I even met one woman in Texas who explained to me that not only did she not use her father's very extensive connections but she wouldn't even consider it. She said, "I'm going to do it on my own."

This idea is comparable to a race car driver at the Indy 500 who wins the pole position and who then says, "I'm going to do it on my own without the advantages of the pole position."

In other words, if you've got 'em, use 'em.

So let's talk about how to develop and utilize your family, social, and business connections. Follow my suggestions in the pages that follow, and, at the least, you'll develop superb replacement names in about six months. Best case, you'll develop and utilize the best list you're likely to see.

Some Industries Built on Connections

It used to be that if you didn't have connections, you wouldn't get hired in some industries. That's how important connections were and are.

This was true in the securities industry, and it was also true in life insurance. As a matter of fact, the life insurance industry today has benefited enormously from the connections of failed agents. Most every insurance company I know has a program called something like Project 100 or Project 200. Before agents are licensed, they are expected to write down the names of one hundred (or two hundred) people they know so that as soon as the license is approved, they can call their connections, get appointments, and sell them something. The problem is that when the agents run out of connections, they are all too often out of business because they don't know how to cold call. And the insurance companies, of course, wind up with the accounts.

So as you can see, I recommend you *start* with cold calling. Let your connections be your second year's business.

136

Why Don't Salespeople Use Connections?

In every industry I've worked in except insurance, I have found that salespeople are reluctant to use connections. In asking countless salespeople why, the answer I hear over and over is, "I just feel awkward," and, "I feel like I'm taking advantage of them." I have a theory on where this awkwardness comes from and, therefore, some ideas on how to overcome it.

The awkwardness comes from the fact that your connections don't perceive you in your new identity. Let's say you grew up in a wealthy family. You are known as the son or daughter of Joe Doakes. You're not recognized as Joe Doakes, account executive, or Joe Doakes, Jr., insurance specialist, or Josephina Doakes, real estate agent. So when you're attempting to communicate to someone from the "wrong identity," it smacks of "taking advantage." And it does create problems. Never mind that many of your connections do a great deal of business with your father at the country club. Never mind that people like doing business with people they know. Because they are not aware of your new identity, they feel awkward and that makes you feel awkward as well. The solution, quite obviously, is to change the way your connections perceive you.

Using Family Connections

Quite obviously, the way to use family connections is to get the family member with the connections to help you. I met an account executive one time whose grandfather was an extremely well-known and influential man in the community. He was active in sports, community affairs, business, and politics. So while the young broker was aggressively cold calling to build an identity of his own, he was following a very low-key approach with the grandfather. The grandfather was making a point of including him on golf foursomes, of inviting him to the country club, of making certain he participated in political meetings, and everywhere he went he took the opportunity of introducing the grandson as, "This is Joe Doakes the third, a stockbroker with Merrill Lynch."

In time, the grandfather's connections would come to perceive

Joe Doakes the third, as Joe Doakes, a stockbroker with Merrill Lynch. And in time, they would begin to discuss investment ideas, and when that occurred, Joe Doakes the third could safely assume that it was okay to be a bit more aggressive in prospecting what are now his grandfather's *and his own* connections.

In my opinion, it is a pity to use connections too soon. You must first alter the perception that people have had of you and create a new perception. And, frankly, this does take some time and effort. So don't try to live on your connections at first. Look at them as next year's business.

Utilizing Your Own Connections

Many people, when coming into a new sales position, know lots of people. These connections may come from college fraternities or sororities, business clubs, former selling jobs, former employers and co-workers, neighbors, and so on. And as with family connections, you are likely to be reluctant to pursue those connections actively as prospects.

The cause of the reluctance is the same. Instead of perceiving you as Joe Doakes, real estate agent, they still know you as Joe Doakes, fraternity brother at Beta Theta Pi, or, Josephina Doakes, copier salesperson at Acme Company. The fraternity brother or copier salesperson has no reason to call his or her friends and talk about real estate, insurance, or whatever.

So the name of the game, once again, is to create a new perception. There is no reason why the old perception as fraternity brother cannot remain in place. But the new perception should become "fraternity brother who is now a real estate broker for Coldwell Banker." Then, when that new perception has been created, you can run with that old truth that "people like doing business with people they know." When your old fraternity brother decides to sell his house, he'll want to call someone he knows who is in the business.

Creating New Perceptions

So how do you create this new perception with your personal connections?

1) Make up your list. Think up *everybody* that might have the need for your services. Review your old address and phone books. Fraternity or sorority directories. Old customer lists. Directories from former employers. Neighbors. Dentist, doctor, lawyer, cleaners, plumbers, TV repair people, home repair professionals, and so on.

2) If at all possible get these names entered in a computer. If you don't have a computer you will have to hand-address the envelopes or type them. Mailing labels are not desirable. These are, after all, your friends, family, and associates. At least treat them with enough respect to address their letter individually.

3) Send your prospects a letter. All you want to do is send them information of general interest to a consumer. Magazine articles are preferable (and generally better written) than company promotion.

The first letter might read like this:

Dear Fred:

As you may recall from the announcement I sent you several months ago, I am now associated with Smither & Snorfleet, insurance agents.

From time to time I will be sending you some material you might find of interest.

If you have any questions by all means give me a call.

Sincerely,

Cortney Blather, 3rd

Send this letter out to all of your connections. Next month send out a similar letter. And the next month something else.

If you're in the securities industry, send along an article on mutual funds or a change in the tax law or what your favorite stock analyst is recommending. You can even print up some notes on small pieces of paper that say, "Here's something I thought you could use." Signed, Joe Doakes. And then all you have to do is initial it. A secretary, sales assistant, or you can then hand-address or type the envelopes; or, if you have access to a computer or word processor, you can have your list input into the memory of the machine, and run the letters and envelopes in a moment's notice.

The new perception might take months to achieve. And when it's done, you'll know it's done because you'll start to get calls. Once you start receiving calls, that's your signal that the new perception is in place. Now you can safely call your connections!

If you persist, you will build a list of people who know who you are and who will contact you when they are interested and ready. Also, by that time you will feel confident that when you contact them, your call will be welcomed. In other words, if you've got the pole position, use it. There is no glamor or magic to being forever condemned to cold calling. And as a matter of fact, if you really analyze the whole cherries and pits theory, you'll see that the style that I'm recommending is really designed to create warm lists. Ultimately, wouldn't it be nice to have connections with a list of fifteen hundred prospects? Well, that's what I'm proposing.

A Canadian Success Story

I was in Rio de Janeiro to give a talk to a group of mutual fund salespeople sponsored by Bolton Tremblay, a major Canadian Mutual Fund. While there, I met a broker from Vancouver who came up after the seminar and told me that there was no way in the world she could ever prospect using my methods. She said that she was absolutely too busy and spent all of her time handling incoming phone calls.

"Where are the calls coming from?" I asked her.

She replied that they were coming from people she had had on her mailing list for eleven years. She said that when she started in the business, whenever she got a name, she would put it on her list and then every six weeks she would send them a research report she had written. She said that after a while the list got so big and so expensive to mail to, that she cut back mailing from every six weeks to every three months. She went on to say that there were people on that list who had been on the list for eleven years and they had never bought anything. Her question was: "Should I take them off the list?"

"Not unless you've got brain damage," I replied.

In other words, I said, "It's working. What you've done is create a list of people who know you, and when they need a financial service they're calling. Don't second-guess the list. Don't try and say because they've been on it three years or eleven years that they should be removed from the list. The list itself is working. It's obviously a good list so leave it alone." Statistics experts tell us that if a population sample is large enough, you can predict the behavior of *the group.* But you can't predict the behavior of an individual within the group. That's why I told this broker to leave the names on the list. The list—the group—was working fine. Because many of the people had been added to her list when she did a seminar for their group, it was generating word of mouth as well as tremendous call-in business. If it ain't broke . . .

At the time I spoke with her, her list was up to eighteen hundred people. It had taken her eleven years to build a list that big. But it doesn't have to take that long. It can be done in a year or less. Now, granted, a year-old list won't be as good as a list you have promoted to for eleven years. But it will work for you. Consider for a moment the people in your call-back file (which I'll discuss in detail in Chapter 8). These are people you have spoken to, made presentations to, gone out to see. They know who you are, and most salespeople never call them or write to them. Too bad. Because they are going to buy something from somebody in the near future. And by staying in touch, whether by phone or by mail, you can earn that business.

Rules for Mailing to Your Connections List

Here are some rules for managing your connections list:

1) Never use mailing labels. Grant your connection the appearance and consideration of *first class.* Either put your connections list in a computer that can individually address envelopes with a letter-quality printer, or hand-address the envelopes.

141

2) Use individual stamps, not metered mail. Again, this is part of creating the look of first class. Something that looks like an individual letter gets opened first.

3) Frequency is more important than brilliance. By this I mean if you don't have anything especially brilliant to say personally to prospects, send them an article about something of interest about your product or service.

4) To be taken off the list, a person must ask to be removed. Otherwise, leave them on the list.

Contacting Your Connections by Phone

When I began working in the securities industry, it was very common to recommend a service approach. The service approach goes like this: "Hello Fred, this is Joe Doakes. As you've probably heard, I'm affiliated now with _____. What I'd like to do is get together with you at the club and take a few minutes and see if there isn't something we can do for you. What time would be best for you?"

This approach works very well with connections. And remember, in its heyday, this approach was *the approach* since only people with connections were hired to begin with. If you don't have connections, you'll have to do it another way. But if you have connections, this is the way to go. Low key. Go see them and don't pressure. (As you saw in Chapter 3, the service approach is most assuredly *not* the way to go with cold prospects. I am including it here for convenience: to keep all the material on prospecting connections in one place. It really is its own separate little subject. And very profitable as well.)

As you plan a connections approach, keep in mind that this is business that will materialize in six months. You can't live on it now.

Assignment: Get enough sources of change lists and referrals flowing in to balance the names falling off your list.

If you have the connections and can use them in your business, dig 'em out and get those envelopes addressed.

8

Managing Your Prospects

We've covered where to get your lists. Now we'll cover how to keep track of them so that you call them when they're supposed to be called and call the best ones first.

It is vital that your name management system be set up early because this prospecting system has the potential of generating a lot of prospect names to follow up. And names get put on paper. And paper has to go somewhere. If it just goes on the desk, it'll get buried. So study this section well and get your name management system set up NOW.

The name of the game is first to *correctly prioritize your lists* and then second, to *spend your available time with your best lists.* For a prospector, name management IS time management.

WARM AND COLD LISTS

Very broadly, we can distinguish between two categories of lists. These are your cold lists and your warm lists. They are managed differently and filed differently.

Your cold lists are those constructed from street directories, corporate directories, and so on. They contain names of people who have not indicated any interest before in your product or service. Your warm lists contain names of people to whom you have spoken who have indicated sufficient level of interest and qualification for you to start a 4 × 6 prospect card. These names are kept in a call-back box.

HOW TO MANAGE LISTS

The Basic Law of List Management is undoubtedly familiar to you:

- "HAVE A PLACE FOR EVERYTHING AND PUT EVERYTHING IN ITS PLACE."

Here is how to do it.

1) Gather up all your lists and put them in one of two piles.

Track down everything. Get the names with scribble marks stashed in your bottom drawer. Get the names you have wrapped around pencils and held in place with a rubber band. And, yes, don't forget the matchbooks at home in your top drawer. Pile them all on top of your desk.

Put all your cold calling lists in one pile.

In the second pile, put all names *that have ever been cherries or greenies.* These are your warm lists.

2) Organize your cold lists.

You'll need a three-ring notebook plus a stack of List Evaluation Sheets (see p. 145). Probably the easiest way to get your List Evaluation Sheets is to photocopy the sample I've given you onto 8½ × 11 paper. You'll also need some tape or rubber cement. Now, paste or tape your list on the space indicated on the List Evaluation Sheet.

There are two reasons why the system is set up this way.

First, by pasting your lists on paper, you have a place to keep notes. As you're calling, you can jot down facts about a particular prospect *while you're talking.* You don't have to stop after the call to write up your card. *You can keep calling!* So organizing your lists in this manner will help you make more calls.

Second, by noting the results of each calling session in the Box Score, you can easily keep track of the lists that are producing three cherries an hour. If you don't keep records on the "good-

LIST EVALUATION SHEET

List Date: _____   **Source:** _____

AREA NO. _____

BOX SCORE

Date:_____ Caller_____
Dials:_____
Contacts:_____
Cherries: _____
Greenies:_____
_____
_____

(paste list here)

BOX SCORE

Date:_____ Caller_____
Dials:_____
Contacts:_____
Cherries: _____
Greenies:_____
_____
_____

BOX SCORE

Date:_____ Caller_____
Dials:_____
Contacts:_____
Cherries: _____
Greenies:_____
_____
_____

BOX SCORE

Date:_____ Caller_____
Dials:_____
Contacts:_____
Cherries: _____
Greenies:_____
_____
_____

ness" of your lists, how will you know which to keep and recycle and which to shred?

Here is how I used the List Evaluation Sheet just recently:

I was test marketing a program I have put together for dentists. I had each street pasted up on my List Evaluation Sheet. The first street I called was a pit street. Sometimes it seems that pits of a feather flock together on the same street. There is no way I would call back that street ever. However, the second street might as well have been from a different planet. I didn't even get through half of it and got four cherries in less than a half-hour. This street will be recalled because I have the records on it.

3) Now, get your warm lists in order.

There is only one way to organize your warm lists into a call-back file: in *date order.*

Here's the reason: The prospecting system described in this book is capable of generating huge numbers of prospects. Consistently using my prospecting system could generate well over one thousand names in a call-back file in less than a year. I know one broker (with Dean Witter) who used my prospecting system for two years and built up over two thousand five hundred names in his call-back box. Needless to say, you can easily manage tens of thousands of names cross-referenced in dozens of ways *if you have access to a personal computer.* If you do not have such access or mastery of it, read on.

If you try to organize hundreds or thousands of names *alphabetically,* you will die in paper. If you organize alphabetically you will, of course, have to develop a second system to know *when* to call those prospects back. This means you will either have to write names down over and over in your calendar or, worse, you will have to maintain *two* cards or sheets of paper on each name—one card for the alphabetical file and the other for the date file.

So why not just keep a date file and eliminate the alphabetical file?

There is only one possible reason not to go ahead and chuck the alphabet file: You're afraid some prospect you spoke to in March will call and tell you she's ready to buy. Since you keep your records in date order, there is no way you can find the information on her quickly. So what is a salesperson to do?

First of all, the chances that someone will call out of the blue and want to buy are slim. But it may happen. So here is what to say:

> Ms. Jones, I keep all my records in date order, and frankly I don't
> have a clue when I have scheduled you for a call-back. Would you
> refresh my memory on the subject of our last conversation?

To set up your date-ordered call-back file system, here's what you need:

1) 4 × 6 (or if you're wordy, 5 × 7) note cards and a box to put them in.

2) 1–31 index. This is just a set of thirty-one index cards, one for each day of the month. Certain prospects, as you'll see shortly, have such a high priority that you'll want to call them back on a particular day. Your 1–31 index enables you to do that.

3) Monthly index. This is a set of twelve index cards, one for each month of the year. Some prospects may not be scheduled for a call-back for months, and this index will help you keep track of them.

4) Colored, pressure-sensitive dots. These are ¾ inch dots that can be used to color-code your call-back file in case you want to be able to cross-reference, say, by area of product interest. If you're a stockbroker, for instance, you might want to let the color blue represent "interested in tax shelters." When you get a good tax shelter offering, you would pull all your "blues" irrespective of which month they're filed in. The color coding system does enable you, then, to cross-reference to other categories without having to start an entirely separate piece of paper on that prospect.

Once you get all the pieces to your call-back file, it's time to take each name in your warm list pile, put it on a 4 × 6 card, and file it correctly. So let's review the different categories of warm lists and where they should be filed in your system.

Your A List

This is the list of people with whom you are in the process of active follow-up. They are the cherries you got as a result of last week's prospecting calls. They may also have come from direct mail leads or telephone inquiries. All your A leads should be "interested and qualified NOW." *This is your best list.*

I will also call your fallback leads A's although they really are not as good as a Grade A cherry. Perhaps we should call them A-minus.

Your A list is not an infinitely large list. In the securities industry, for example, you cannot possibly follow up on more than fifty

147

people a week. In insurance, it's more like twenty-five. In real estate, more than ten and you are very busy.

> *FILING PRINCIPLE:* FILE A-GRADE PROSPECTS IN THE 1–31 FILE ONLY. SCHEDULE YOUR CHERRIES FOR A CALL-BACK IN ONE WEEK BY FILING THEM 5 BUSINESS DAYS FROM THE DATE OF INITIAL CONTACT. FILE YOUR FALLBACKS AHEAD TWO WEEKS. DO NOT PUT ANY OTHER TYPE OF PROSPECT IN THAT FILE. No B's, no C's, no birthday reminders, nothing. By ONLY putting A's in the 1–31 file, you'll have easily separated your most important names from all the hundreds or thousands of others you have. Keep them separate!

Your B List

This is the list of people who will be interested or qualified at a known, later date. It's the green cherry list I mentioned in Chapter 2, and if you correctly qualify for interest and money on the first call, *this will be your second-best list.*

> *FILING PRINCIPLE:* FILE B-GRADE PROSPECTS IN THE FRONT PART OF THE MONTHLY SLOT. IF YOUR PROSPECT SAID HE OR SHE WILL BE ABLE TO MAKE A DECISION IN MARCH, CALL IN FEBRUARY. I say "front part" because we're going to put something else in the back part of the monthly file.

Your C List

In many industries, this list is the most neglected. So what is the C list?

The C list is your "pitch and miss list," the list of people you have made a presentation to *and didn't sell.* Many salespeople operating in "unlimited markets"—stockbrokers, insurance agents, and so on—actually throw this list away.

Suppose you are a real estate agent and you find that the Joneses are thinking of selling their house. You set up an appointment and go see them. Suppose further that the appointment does not produce a listing, and they tell you they are going to make up their minds about moving sometime next year.

This meets our definition of "made a presentation and didn't sell." Therefore, this is a C-Grade prospect, a "pitch and miss," or P&M as some people call them. The great advantage to this list is: they know you. (Please don't confuse the C list with pits. Pits, if you recall, are just kept on your cold calling list. You keep calling the cold calling list as long as it's a good list.)

Why are we keeping this list? I can give you all kinds of philosophical arguments. But how about this one: because it's the third best list you will ever develop. If you just *maintain periodic contact* with these prospects, you'll eventually get the business.

There is, however, a big problem with the C list, and it probably explains why so many salespeople throw away their C list. It's this:

THEY KNOW YOU. AND THEREFORE THEY TALK TO YOU. YOU, BEING A SALESPERSON, TALK TOO MUCH. AND THE LIST ISN'T GOOD ENOUGH TO WARRANT TWENTY-MINUTE PHONE CALLS!

FILING PRINCIPLE: FILE C PROSPECTS IN THE BACK OF THE MONTHLY DIVIDER TWO TO THREE MONTHS AFTER EACH CONTACT. In other words, you're going to recycle your C list every two to three months. By filing it in the back of a monthly slot, you keep it separate from the B list, which is filed in the front.

THE LIST MANAGEMENT SYSTEM IN ACTION

So you can see this system in action, let's follow a prospect from cold call to the opening of an account.

Let's say you're a computer salesperson. You are cold calling a list of engineers. After you have opened your conversation, it goes like this:

YOU: Mr. Jones, this computer leases for $855 per month. If you did like it, would that amount pose a problem for you at this particular time?

JONES: Yes, it would.

YOU: Okay. Since this is the computer you need, I don't want to recommend a less expensive one. Tell me, when will you be able to handle an $855 a month payment?

149

JONES: Just as soon as we handle a couple of tax problems. We should be in shape, say, in May.

YOU: Great! Suppose I give you a call then, okay?

You have just added a terrific name to your B list.

Let's make a prospect card on Jones and file him in the front part of our April slot. He's a B. Jot down name, address, phone number and any other important information that may have come from your conversation.

Now it's April. It's time to call him back. When you call your greenie list, go straight for an appointment. Here's your call in April.

YOU: Hi, Mr. Jones. Ralph Norton over here at Acme Computer. When we spoke last March, you mentioned you would be interested in considering our computer again after you handled some tax problems. I have to be out your way next Thursday, and I would like to stop by and see you. I have a spot available at 9:00 A.M. and another one open at 4:00. Which of those would be better for you?

JONES: Well, Ralph, that tax problem has gotten worse. I just am not in a situation now to make that kind of commitment.

YOU: When would you expect to have everything under control?

JONES: Hard to say, really.

YOU: Okay. Suppose I just check back with you from time to time. Meantime, if anything comes up, you've still got my card, right?

Now what are we going to do with Jones? He's not an A. And he's certainly not a B. After all, he doesn't meet our definition "interest with money available at known later date." So let's downgrade him to a C and file him in the back part of the June slot.

Now it's June. It's time to call Jones again.

The basic principle in handling your C list is to always qualify for available funds first. Remember, Jones knows you. Find out about the money *first.*

YOU: Hi! Ralph Norton. Acme Computer. I'm just touching base with you to see if you got that tax problem sorted out and might be interested in using our new computer to help you keep track of all the money you're making?

JONES: Funny you should call. I got a call from my CPA this morning. He says we don't owe a dime!

YOU: That's great! I have to be out your way tomorrow afternoon. I have a spot at 2:00 and another one again at 3:30. Which one looks better to you?

JONES: Let's make it 3:30.

Jones now gets upgraded to an A. If today is June 15, drop his card in the "16" slot in your 1–31 file. Let's assume you get the sale. Remove his name entirely from your call-back box. His name now belongs with your customer records, which should be maintained *in an entirely separate system.*

Using Your Name Management System

Come to work in the morning. If it's early, take out a cold-calling list and pound out an hour's worth of cold calls. It will get the juices going. At the end of the hour, take note of the results you've recorded on your List Evaluation Sheet.

Now, pull out your A file for today. If you are keeping the system correctly, there should be some A's in there to call. Call them for appointments. Your A file should ALWAYS be good for some appointments or business (if not, you've misfiled). By getting that appointment first thing in the morning, count on receiving a boost to your morale.

Next, let's call some B's. Call as many as you can from your current month's B file. You'll set some more appointments from these.

Then go to work on your C's. If you have a big C file for the month, you may not have to do much cold calling. Remember,

151

the objective of this system is to minimize your cold calling. Hopefully, by now you'll see that after a few months of it, your cold calling will probably be limited to replacing names that are removed from your call-back box. By this time, many of your cold lists won't be all that cold either. You will have cycled through them several times and the people on them will know you.

HOW TO EVALUATE YOUR LISTS

To evaluate means: to fix the value of. To know which lists to spend your time with, you do need to be able to evaluate them.

I have actually already given you a general evaluation system for your call-back file. The A list is your best. Next comes B and then C. And finally your cold lists. But suppose you've made a mistake. Or suppose your C list is really worse than your cold lists, how will you know? What's needed is a way to tell how good is good. And the standard is already given in your definition of a good list. In Chapter 6, I defined a *Good* list as "any list that will generate a minimum of three cherries per hour."

So we'll evaluate every list *but the A list* in terms of cherries per hour. The A list, of course, requires a different standard since it is made up entirely of cherries. We'll evaluate the A list according to a more conventional "conversion rate" standard. In other words, how many A's convert into accounts?

So let's look at your warm and cold lists to find out how long it takes to find one cherry. Unless you are rich, your primary investable resource in building a sales career is time, not money. If you spend money, say on a mailing, you want to know how much one cherry costs. If you spend time, you naturally want to know *how much time a cherry costs.* According to my definition of a good list (three cherries per hour), a cherry should cost you no more than twenty minutes.

This does not mean, however, that you should throw out any list that won't produce three cherries per hour. You might replace a list producing two cherries per hour with one that does .005. So, keep what you've got *while you look for something better.*

The Upgrading Process

Let's say you're the new salesperson on the block. The only lists you have are the Yellow Pages, some street address lists, a manufacturer's guide, and a set of old prospect cards some failed salesperson left lying around. Very simply, here is how to evaluate a list.

Call for an hour and record how many cherries you get. If you get three, your time cost per cherry is twenty minutes.

Here are some results from your initial tests on your first collection of 1500 names.

Street Address Lists:	2.5 cherries per hour.
Manufacturer's Guide:	1.2 cherries per hour.
Old Prospect Cards:	0.8 cherries per hour
Attorneys (Yellow Pages):	0.005 cherries per hour.

This averages out to 1.12 cherries per hour. To put it another way, a cherry costs you 54 minutes of time.

To upgrade your results or cut your time cost per cherry—get rid of the attorneys and get a better list.

Let's say you go out and get a corporate directory. After applying our test procedure to it, your results are as follows:

Acme Company Directory:	3.3 cherries per hour.
Street Address Lists:	2.5 cherries per hour.
Manufacturer's Guide:	1.2 cherries per hour.
Old Prospect Cards:	0.8 cherries per hour.

If you have done what Shakespeare said, "first kill the attorneys," you now average 1.95 cherries per hour which means that one cherry costs you 30.7 minutes. In time cost, that's a *fifty-six percent cost cut!!*

Once again, weed from the bottom. Get another list. Test it. If it's better than the Old Prospect Cards list, throw that one away and once again, you'll have cut your time cost per prospect.

After you have been in business several months, your B and C lists will have come onstream. Here are some possible results.

B List	4.2 cherries per hour.
C List	3.8 cherries per hour.
Acme Company Directory	3.2 cherries per hour.
Street Address Lists	2.6 cherries per hour.

Here you are averaging almost 4 cherries per hour and your time cost is down to almost 15 minutes. So the longer you work the system and the more you improve your lists, the less you have to worry about because you are getting almost three times as many prospects per unit of invested time as you were when you started. This is POWER!

QUESTIONS AND ANSWERS ABOUT LISTS

Here are some questions about lists that I know you have on your mind. Or, if you don't, you should.

Q: How long should I leave a name on one of my cold-calling lists?

A: Don't think in terms of a "name." Remember, prospecting as a subject deals with *groups of people.* As long as the *list itself* is good, leave it on the list. When you can replace the list with a better list, throw them all out.

Q: But what about jerks?

A: Grab them by the chain and haul them off your list. Dig them out of your call-back file and out of your account book if necessary. Technically, I suppose this contradicts my answer to the previous question which said pits should be left on the list. A jerk, however, is not just another kind of pit. He or she is something else entirely. And if you know you have a list with a bunch of jerks on it, the chances of your continuing to "recycle" that list are somewhere between zero and nothing. So throw them out.

Q: How long should someone remain on the C list?

A: If someone is *correctly qualified to begin with,* we do not evaluate individual names except as follows:

　　a) If your C list is producing three cherries an hour or better, don't mess with it.

　　b) If it falls below three an hour or if other cold-calling lists are producing more than three, weed it down. By that I mean go through it and take out everyone that you have even the slightest bad feeling for.

Q: If someone is not interested when I cold call them, what should I write down?

A: Nothing. Why prejudice your list?

Q: Do I have to call someone if I don't want to?

A: No.

Q: What's the best list to get?

A: One that takes you a lot of effort and time.

Q: What is a false cherry?

A: It's a pit that wears a vinyl cherry skin. It's someone you qualify as a cherry and then find out he or she is neither interested nor qualified. You'll generally identify these on your second call. They'll never come to the phone, will brush you off, and were really pits that momentarily sounded like cherries. So just return them to the list from which they came. Don't let them in your call-back box.

A FINAL WORD ON LISTS

I have said more about lists in this book than I have said or will say about any other topic. The topic is as important as I have stressed. Somewhere between ten and forty hours of slogging work developing good lists will pay you for the rest of your career.

Go for it!

155

9

How You Sound

Some years ago I was doing a seminar for an insurance company in San Diego. As I walked around the room listening to everyone call, I couldn't help but notice one agent who, in all truth, sounded as if he was sucking on a lemon. And not only did he sound that way, his facial expression was curled into a sneer. He really sounded as if he didn't like the people he was talking to, and guess what? They didn't like him either. While everyone else in the room was getting excellent results, his results, like his sound, sucked lemons.

Our conversation went like this:

BILL: Fred, I want you to smile when you talk.

FRED: But I don't feel like smiling.

BILL: I don't recall asking what you felt like.

FRED: Well, I still don't feel like smiling.

BILL: All right. Here's what I want you to do. I want you to smile anyway. It will change the sound of your voice whether you feel like it or not. And since people can't see you, who cares if you look like a cat from *Alice in Wonderland,* sitting on a limb just grinning?

After that exchange, I asked around and came up with an oversized make-up mirror. I propped it up on his desk, and made him smile into the mirror. I really didn't care if he felt like smiling or not. I knew if he would physically put a smile on his face, it would change the way he sounded. And the response he would get from his improved sound would change the way he felt. If you want to prove this to yourself, simply read this paragraph into a tape recorder. Scowl as you read. Now paste a smile on. Read it again. Listen to them both. You will hear that putting a smile on your face puts one in your voice.

Our scowling insurance agent picked up several appointments that night . . . but not until he put a smile on his face.

Developing the "right sound" can mean the difference between success or failure. If you sound friendly, sound as though you know what you're talking about, speak at the right speed, and don't sound as if you're reading, you can succeed—especially if you have your list, script, and volume of calls under control. If you sound singsongy, bored, sour, too fast, too slow, or wishy-washy, you might as well go apply for a bookkeeping job. Once you get someone on the phone, all of your other good points—your good dress, your good looks, the way you sit and gesture—aren't worth a bucket of water in a rainstorm. After all, they can't see you, they can't see your bright eyes, your nice dress, your expressions. All they can do is hear you. So all you have in your favor is what you say and how you say it. That's all.

So let's talk about the elements that make up the "right sound": voice inflection, pacing, emphasis, speed, and enthusiasm. Perfecting these elements of speech will "un-can" any "canned pitch." If you correctly use the five elements discussed in this chapter, your presentation won't ever sound as if it's being read.

VOICE INFLECTION

Perhaps there should be a law in sales that reads "Certainty Sells." For our purposes, let's define "certainty" as "sounding as if you know what you're talking about." If you are new in the business, you undoubtedly are *not certain* of many things. But your survival depends on sounding as if you are not only certain, but are a veteran.

I could write pages on the people I have met who never made it because they didn't sound as if they had a clue whether they were in Mexico or whether it was Tuesday. One stockbroker I knew had an incredibly successful system of picking stocks. The few clients he had had done extremely well. But he had such a severe case of stage fright that he couldn't tell his story without sounding like a brand new kid on the block. Consequently, he couldn't convince people he was telling the truth when he told them about his system. And he washed out of the business.

There are three elements involved in creating certainty. Perhaps most important is having a product to sell that you understand, can explain, and most important, *believe in.* Second, you need to have a script that is effective. Third, you need to be able to deliver your script with correct voice inflection. There's not much I can do for you here on your product. And we've already covered the subject of scripts. So let's talk about voice inflection as a very important element of developing certainty.

To give you a good idea of what voice inflection is, I want you to sing aloud the following song:

Twinkle twinkle little <u>star</u> how I wonder where you <u>are.</u>

I have underlined two words, "star" and "are." The word "star" was at a higher *pitch* than the word "are." Pitch simply refers to highness or lowness of the voice. A high C on the piano has a much higher pitch than a middle C.

Now that you know what pitch means, let's define "inflection." Inflection is defined as a change in pitch the voice makes in speaking a word, phrase, or sentence. A person speaking in a monotone would have no variation in pitch. To get a good idea of the word monotone, simply sing our little song here without changing pitch.

Inflection is very important as a speech element because of what pressure, fear, and anxiety do to it. People who normally sound like red-blooded human beings change their voice inflection when they are afraid or nervous. And not surprisingly, this change makes them sound afraid and nervous. As you read further, please keep in mind that you may *feel nervous* when you call. But I am going to try and help you *sound confident.* As people respond to your confident sound, your feelings of fear and anxiety will dissolve.

I am going to introduce some marks in your text here to indicate direction of voice inflection. An up arrow (↑) means that the voice goes up on that word. A down arrow (↓) means that the voice goes down on that word. Now, in the English language, if you want to make a statement of fact, your voice will drop slightly at the end of the sentence. Please read aloud the sentence below. With a down arrow (↓) I have shown what should happen to the pitch of your voice.

My name is Fred Smithers. (↓)

If you read that sentence correctly, your voice dropped slightly on the last syllable of the word "Smithers." If you walked up to a stranger and said, "My name is Fred Smithers (↓)," he would believe you. *Correct inflection creates belief.*

Now let's take another example. If you ask a question, your pitch goes up on an important word in the sentence. Please read aloud the question below. (If you don't do these exercises aloud, it's very difficult for me to make the points I'm trying to make. So do follow along.)

Is your name Fred Smithers (↑)?

If you read this one correctly your voice would have lilted up at the end of the sentence. The person whom you were addressing would have clearly responded to it as a question, and if his name was Fred Smithers, he would have said, "Yes, it is."

Let's take a final example. If you wish to issue a command, your voice drops sharply at the end of a sentence. I want you to imagine that you have a sixteen-year-old daughter. You've just inspected her room, and you find that it looks like the Russian army has only recently decamped. As you look closer you see that what you thought was a pile of dirty clothes sipping a soda all by itself is actually your daughter. She's listening to a tape recorder, watching TV, and talking on the phone at the same time. Read aloud the command below. Emphasize the word "room" with a hard drop in your inflection.

Nicci, clean up your room (↓)!

If you read this one correctly, your voice would have dropped sharply on the word "room," and she would certainly have known that she had better do it right now.

Now let's take a look at some common inflection mistakes. Imagine the same situation with your daughter's room. Instead of inflecting down on the word room, I want you to read it aloud and inflect up. Take what should be a command and make it a question with an up-inflection. So here goes.

Nicci, clean up your room (↑)?

If you read this one as I indicated, there is little doubt that Nicci will respond, "Sure Dad. (↑) How about tomorrow?"(↑)

And thus what should have come across as a command from parent to daughter comes across as a wimpish request and gets a mushy response. (And certainly no clean room!)

Let's take a look at a more common inflection mistake. Let's inflect what should come across as a statement of fact like a question. I want you to read the line below aloud with inflection marks as shown.

Good morning (↑). My name is Fred Smithers (↑). I work over here at Acme Company (↑).

If you read this one with the voice inflecting up as shown, you certainly sounded like a world-class wimp. And yet, without your being fully aware of it, the chances are at least fifty-fifty that this is how you sound on the phone. If you inflect up on the last syllable of your last name and your company name, it appears that you don't know who you are or where you work. And this lets people know right from the very first instant you open your mouth that you are brand new to the position *whether you are or not!* And who wants to have a new salesperson practice on them? Frankly, some people will take a minute out of their day to squash a wimpy salesman just as they would an annoying bug.

If you want to conduct an interesting test, open the White Pages to the "Joneses" or "Smiths" or whatever. Using your worst inflection, call the "Jones" column and read the script below. See if you can get anyone interested at all. Here's your script.

May I speak to M/M _____ Jones please (↑)? M/M _____ Jones (↑) this is Fred Smithers (↑). I work over here at Acme Company (↑). We are selling gold coins at half price (↑). Are you interested (↑)?

Typically, if you inflect the script as I've marked it, you will sound very hesitant and uncertain. You will find that not only will people not be interested in your offer, but they will *act as if they didn't hear you.* Apparently, your own uncertainty is such that it clouds theirs, and they won't believe what they thought they heard because they aren't even sure they heard it. Evidently, *uncertainty creates disbelief.* To create belief, first believe it yourself, and then sound like you believe it. If you let the anxiety of making the call force you into sounding like you don't know what you are talking about, you will cause your prospect to feel uncertain as well.

What I'd like you to do right now is read aloud the script below into a tape recorder. Listen back. Did you get the correct inflection?

Good morning (↓). This is (your name) (↓) with (your company name) (↓). You know who we are (↓), don't you (↑)?

Avoid sounding wimpish. Use correct inflection (↓). (That was a command!)

If you have been following my directions so far, you will have already written yourself a script. What you should now do is go through that script and mark it up with up arrows and down arrows for correct voice inflection. Make absolutely certain that your name and company name are inflected correctly. (You'll want a ↓ on the last syllable of your last name and a ↓ on the last syllable of your company name.)

PACING

Let's add another speech element. We'll call it pacing. Let's define "pacing" as simply the insertion of space between words. To dramatize this, read aloud the passage below:

Good morning. This is Fred Smithers. I'm calling to let you know that you will receive a check in the mail for one million dollars.

Now certainly that would get someone's attention. Now read it again. This time, make a slight pause everywhere you see a "/" mark. This indicates a very slight amount of space. Keep playing with it until it sounds natural.

> Good morning./ This is Fred Smithers. /I'm calling to let you know that you will receive a check in the mail/for one / million / dollars.

If you read it correctly this time, you would have added a lot of impact to some already strong words. Marking your script up for pacing is the best way I know to force yourself to slow down.

Can you guess which newscaster has made exaggerated pacing his hallmark? Paul Harvey, of course:

> Good morning, Americans./// Stand-by// for//news!

Paul Harvey is the highest paid broadcaster in radio. Next time you hear him on the radio, listen to his pacing.

Below, I have taken some of the lines from the scripts I've used as examples and shown how I would mark them both for inflection and pacing. To get a good idea of the flow and rhythm, you should read each of them straight through with no pacing. And then read them through leaving some little spaces at the points indicated.

> M/M _____, I have some very important information for you on a guaranteed / investment. It's a bank CD and it's paying / _____ / percent. Could I send you some information on our terms and rates?

> I have some important information on how to get a higher rate of return on your money than a CD. The interest compounds. Uncle Sam doesn't touch it / at tax time. And if something should happen to you, your family would get a whole / bunch / of money. Could I send you some information on it?

> M/M _____, I have some very interesting information for you on how our cellular phone can save you time, money, and possibly / keep you out of trouble with your (HUSBAND/WIFE) if you're going to be late. Could I send it to you?

EMPHASIS

Let's define emphasis as stress on a particular word or phrase. By putting emphasis on words, you communicate importance. Read aloud the paragraph below with no emphasis:

Good morning. This is Fred Smithers. I'm calling to let you know that you will receive a check in the mail for one million dollars.

We'll use an underline to indicate emphasis on a word. Now read the same passage again, this time with emphasis.

Good morning. This is Fred Smithers. I'm calling to let you know that you will receive a check in the mail for <u>one</u> <u>million</u> <u>dollars</u>.

Below, I have added an emphasis to some of our script lines that we used above but which previously only had pacing. Read each of them aloud with correct emphasis:

M/M _____, I have some <u>very</u> important information for you on a guaranteed / investment. It's a bank CD and it's paying / _____ / percent. Could I send you some information on our terms and rates?

I have some important information on how to get a <u>higher</u> rate of return on your <u>money</u> than a CD. The interest compounds. Uncle Sam doesn't touch it / at tax time. And if something should happen to you, your family would get a whole / bunch / of money. Could I send you some information on it?

M/M _____, I have some very interesting information for you on how our cellular phone can save you time, money and <u>possibly</u> / keep you out of trouble with your husband/wife if you're going to be late. Could I send it to you?

SPEED OF TALKING

Certainly one problem with a written script is that people tend to read too fast. And that is a big problem because a rapid-fire rate of speech is associated with H I G H   P R E S S U R E. And we certainly don't want that.

So how fast should you talk?

About the same rate as your prospect. If you call up someone

163

who just moved to Texas from Manhattan, don't lay down a "good ole boy" Good Evening. Hedoesn'thavetime.

So concentrate on listening to rate of speech. And practice tracking with it. The best help you can get is to tape record yourself and listen to your rate of speech and that of the prospect.

ENTHUSIASM

Since the beginning of time, sales trainers have preached enthusiasm as a sure-fire tool in sales. In sales, after all, we are going to *motivate* someone to do something different from what he or she is now doing. And to motivate, you have to use energy.

I learned this lesson in my very first sales job which, as I mentioned in the Introduction, was selling dictionaries door-to-door for Southwest Publishing Company. My crew leader, an old family friend named Buzz, really knew only two things about sales. The first one was:

"Bill, I want you out there running from door to door."

I used to tell him, "Buzz, you've lost your mind. For twenty-three days in a row it's been over one hundred degrees. If I get out there and run door to door, I'll die from dehydration and salt loss. I'll walk fast, but that's the best I'll do."

The second thing he knew about sales was, "Good, I want you out there being enthusiastic."

My response, never directly to him, was, "Sure, Buzz. It's real easy to be enthusiastic to some of these 'blue hairs' that I meet at eight o'clock in the morning when I've just dragged my tail out of bed and thrown it out on the street."

Well, one day, I was walking down the street, trying to be warm and friendly, and Buzz came tearing around the corner in an old brown Valiant of his that sounded as if it needed a muffler job. He jumped out of the car, sprinted across the yard, grabbed me by the wrist, and we went running down the street to the next house. I knocked on the door, some lady came to the door, I went through my pitch, and she didn't buy anything.

BUZZ: Good, you sound dead.

GOOD: Buzz! I'm trying to sound warm and friendly.

BUZZ: Warm and friendly? I never said anything to you about being warm and friendly. I said I wanted you to be out there being enthusiastic. I want you to wake these people up. They are asleep at the wheel.

GOOD: Buzz, I don't feel enthusiastic.

BUZZ: (scratching his head) I don't recall that I even asked you what you felt like. As a matter of fact, ask me how much I care. I don't care if you feel terrible. But in my sales crew, you're not going to sound any of this warm and friendly nonsense. You're going to sound enthusiastic. I want you out there being enthusiastic. As a matter of fact, if you'll just act enthusiastic, you'll start to feel that way.

I'd heard it before. To feel enthusiastic, ACT enthusiastic. On and on and on. That's all I ever heard from the guy.

So, just to prove him wrong, I went to the house next door, knocked, and some lady who looked as if she had just stuck her finger in a light socket answered the door.

"Hi!" I said in my most enthusiastic tone. She sort of shook her head, focused her eyes, saw me out there with a big smile on my face, and said, "Oh, hi!"

And I went right into my presentation with a big smile pasted on my face. "We are showing this new book in town. Have you heard about it?" And then I stuck out the book so that she had to grab it.

She said, "No, I haven't."

I said, "Let me tell you about it." And I sold her a book.

And then I tried it again, and very shortly I was selling two books an hour, which was up from one book every two hours. So my sales went up four hundred percent as a result of moving quickly and being enthusiastic.

It is true. Genuine enthusiasm will almost wake the dead. If you don't have it genuinely, act as if you have it and then you'll feel it.

ASSIGNMENT

1) Mark up your own script for inflection, pacing, and emphasis.

2) Read it aloud without any of these elements.

3) Read it into a tape recorder with correct inflection. Listen back. Keep working at it until you have the inflection right. It's not a bad idea to get someone else to listen to you. Sometimes people will have a hard time hearing their own inflection mistakes.

4) Now read it with correct inflection *and* pacing. Use your tape recorder.

5) Add emphasis.

6) And finally, enthusiasm. Wake 'em up, tiger!

10

How to Make More Calls

You cannot be a cherry picker on fifteen dials an hour. There is only one exception to the rule, and we can deal with it right now.

If you have an absolutely outstanding list, you don't have to, indeed can't, make the large volume of calls required on average or even better-than-average lists.

I have seen lists in the securities industry, in real estate, computers, and long distance telephone, that are so good that the people you are calling take up a lot of time because they ask questions and otherwise get involved. They want to talk. You cannot, therefore, make lots of calls. But who cares *if you are getting three cherries an hour.*

With this one exception: With an outstanding list, you cannot cherry pick on just a few calls an hour. Why? Because there simply aren't enough cherries. The competition got there first.

SALES IS A NUMBERS GAME, BUT . . .

Anyone who has been around sales longer than one day has heard someone say, "Sales is a numbers game."

This is very true. And the assumption is that sales is an "arithmetical numbers game." For those who don't remember what an "arithmetical progression" is, study the graph on page 168.

What this graph says is just common sense. It says if you double your number of calls, you will double your number of prospects per hour. It is also not true.

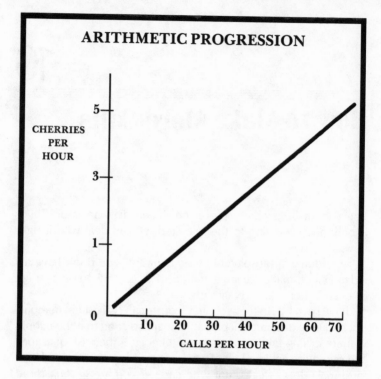

ARITHMETIC PROGRESSION

CHERRIES
PER
HOUR

CALLS PER HOUR

Yes, sales is a numbers game. But it is not an "arithmetic" game. It's "geometric" and is represented by a type of graph called a geometrical progression, pictured on the facing page.

This graph says that if you double your calls per hour from ten to twenty, don't expect much change in results. As a matter of fact, it says that you will get more results *per hour* when you increase your dials from forty to sixty than you got when you doubled them from twenty to forty.

Sales *is a numbers game.* But most people don't push it far enough to reap the benefits.

Why these dramatic increases in results after about forty calls an hour? I think the reason for this has to do most of all with attitude.

At fifteen dials an hour, you're not finding much. You're hungry. When you perceive even a flicker of interest in a prospect, you tend to hang onto it desperately. And I am sure you know that a

168

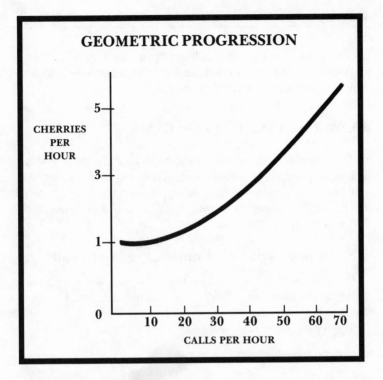

GEOMETRIC PROGRESSION

CHERRIES PER HOUR

CALLS PER HOUR

prospect can sniff out a hungry salesperson at one hundred yards, and at the first whiff they're gone just as surely as a deer will bolt at the scent of a lion.

However, when your calls per hour are cranked up past forty or fifty, you have such an abundance of people to talk to that the value of any one person who rejects you is very low. This is just the law of supply and demand used to determine the value of any one prospect. The greater the supply of prospects, the lower the value of any one of them. And the lower the value, the less you worry when you lose one. When one rejects you, who cares? You have so many to deal with you can't possibly care about any one call.

The best way to handle feeling hungry is to eat. The best way to handle prospect hunger is to talk to lots of prospects. This may sound too simple, but I assure you there is great magic in it. By concentration on numbers, you don't worry about results. By not worrying about results, you will get them much more easily.

With this principle in mind, let's go ahead and take a look at how to generate large numbers of calls.

HOW TO MAKE LOTS OF DIALS

The best way to show you how to make a lot of calls, is to show you how to get rid of wasted time. When you've done that, you will find your number of calls increases dramatically. No one of the principles outlined below will revolutionize your business. All of them taken together will.

Always have your next number ready to call

Some years ago, I spent some time observing some insurance agents as they worked. I simply stood around and watched them call.

The typical work flow went like this:

Find the number of someone to call.

Call it.

Talk to the prospect.

Hang up the phone.

Find the next number.

Pick up the phone.

Dial the number.

This took forever. Anyone watching could see that a great amount of time was lost in the simple act of hanging up the phone between calls. Why were the agents hanging up between calls? Simple. They had to find their next number.

Therefore my first principle is: **Always have your next number ready to call.** To show you how to do this, we'll do a little exercise right here on the spot.

Below, I have created a fictitious list from South Street in your city. Look it over and then continue reading and then I'll tell you what to do.

170

South Street

101	Jones, R. D.	437–2351
102	Smith, J. S.	427–3483
103	Brown, K. W.	487–9132
104	King, M. J.	582–6159
105	Doe, J. A.	498–2898
106	Edwards, M. D.	421–5694
107	Thomas, G. K.	527–2782
108	Simpson, F. R.	542–8352
109	White, S. W.	453–4694
110	James, C. T.	598–7138

Get a business card or other straight edge. Put it so that you can only read the name of Jones, R. D., at 101 South Street.

Put your hand up by your ear as if you're making a phone call. Dial the number on an imaginary phone. The minute you imagine the phone number starting to ring, move your straight edge down so you can see the next number. All the names except Jones and Smith should be covered by your straight edge.

101	Jones, R. D.	437–2351
102	Smith, J. S.	427–3483

So here is the principle when using a street address or similar list:

1) Put a straight edge under your first name and number.

2) Dial it.

3) The instant it starts to ring, pull your straight edge down *so you can see the next number.*

In our example above, you are talking to Jones. When Jones tells you he's not interested, you glance down just above your straight edge and see the name Smith, J. S. While leaving the phone at your ear, you disconnect Jones and immediately dial Smith. If Smith answers, you've got one hand to hold the phone and the other hand to take notes *while you're talking to Smith.*

The instant Smith starts to ring, you pull your straight edge down so you can now see Brown.

By following this simple procedure, you never have to put

171

down the phone between calls. And by leaving the phone at your ear, you just bought yourself ten to twelve extra calls per hour.

If you keep your prospect names on note cards, the principle is slightly different. Here's how it works.

Take a stack of cards and put them on your desk in front of you. With your hand at your ear as in the previous example, dial the top number on your imaginary phone.

The instant that number starts to ring, pull the top card down in front of the pile so you can read the name and number of the next prospect.

As you attempt to implement this principle with either cards or lists, you may find you tend to get confused and call the same person twice. If you blow it, don't worry. Rally with the cry of a cherry picker, thankyouverymuch, and disconnect.

Never hang up the phone!

When salespeople hang up the phone, they tend to do something else.

I watched a stockbroker the other day. He made a call. Hung up the phone. Put something on his stock quote terminal. Rummaged around on his desk for something. Took out a research report. Looked at that for a moment. Said something to the broker next to him. And finally made another phone call.

When you're prospecting, you'll pick a lot of extra cherries by *never hanging up the phone.* If you followed my recommendations in Chapter 8 and pasted your cold-calling lists on List Evaluation Sheets, you won't have to stop to write down the prospect's name, address, and phone number. You'll just draw a circle around your cherry's name and jot down any other notes right there on the List Evaluation Sheet. You won't even stop to make up prospect cards or address envelopes. You'll do that at the end of an hour when you take a short break. By isolating similar actions into their own units of time, you develop speed and velocity at each.

As an aside, those who do a lot of calling each and every day would do well to invest in a headset. The headset eliminates the requirement most companies have that their salespeople receive an operation every three months to surgically remove the phone receiver from the ear.

Let the phone ring four times and disconnect

Some years ago, I was told by a representative of Pacific Telephone that eighty-five percent of the people who are home will answer on or before the fourth ring. So what are the other fifteen percent doing? Who knows? But we do know they don't want to come to the phone. If they had wanted to come to the phone they would have got there earlier. So we can say with a fair amount of confidence that the people who do come to the phone after the fourth ring are not a very high-grade prospect.

There is an exception. If you are calling a retirement community, allow up to six rings, since the people you are calling may not be as fast as younger people.

If you are calling businesses during the day, I can promise you that if you allow the phone to ring six times, and someone does finally answer, it will be some harried receptionist who will say to you, "Good morning, Acme Company, hold please." And you'll be listening to some "easy listenin' " station.

Don't stay on hold forever

In most companies with more than ten employees, the first person who answers the phone is called the receptionist. Normally, the receptionist does not screen calls. It's this person's job to simply route calls to the correct extension.

This brings us to the fact that there are two places you can get put on hold. The first is, of course, with the receptionist. You call for Ms. Jones, and in the process of being connected to her office, you get put on hold. I would not stay on this type of hold longer than about twenty seconds.

The second place you may get put on hold is after you have spoken to the secretary who is now going to put you through to the boss. Since in daytime calling it can be very difficult to reach people, you can afford to invest a bit more time in waiting to talk to your decision maker. I would give it about a minute. And then simply disconnect and go on to your next number.

173

Don't write down negatives

Don't write down who is not in, who is not interested, or any other "nots." It's a waste of time. Simply recycle these lists again in six weeks. If you call the lists back today or tomorrow, and try to reach those same people, you'll be calling a list of people who, in the current time period, *are NOT.* Who cares what they are not being or doing? Right now they are just NOT.

I know one salesman who literally went out of the business because he violated this principle. He would call through a list and talk to those he could speak with. He would very carefully note down those who were not in, and so forth. Then he would turn around and call the list again. His contact rate on the second cycle through the list would worsen. However, he would still be able to reach some people. Not being one to quit, he would then call all those who had not been in on the second cycle through the list. By this time, he was really down to the hard core of people who are NOT. And he was wondering all along why he was having such trouble getting people to the phone. By writing down the negatives and then calling prospects back *in the current time frame,* he created a NOT-list. Don't do it.

Also, writing down negatives prejudices the list. Suppose you were given a list to call that said, "Not interested, not home, busy, and so on and so on." Would you want to call it? Writing down negatives prejudices the list when the time does come to call it back in six weeks or so.

Take no call-back information from non-decision makers.

Let's define a couple of terms here. By "call-back information," I mean information as to when Mr. Jones or Mrs. Smith will be in. By "non-decision maker" I mean secretaries, receptionists, and in some markets, wives or husbands.

Here is an example of what happens when you try and get call-back information from a non-decision maker.

YOU: *Ring, ring.*

SECRETARY: Good morning, Mr. Jones's office.

YOU:	I'd like to speak to Mr. Jones. Is he in?
SECRETARY:	May I tell him who's calling?
YOU:	This is Fred Smithers.
SECRETARY:	And what's your company?
YOU:	Acme Company.
SECRETARY:	Will he know you?
YOU:	No, but he should.
SECRETARY:	Just a moment please. (pause) I'm sorry, he's not available at the moment.
YOU:	When do you expect him?
SECRETARY:	He'll be tied up in meetings most of the day.
YOU:	Well, can I call him back tomorrow morning?
SECRETARY:	You can certainly try.
YOU:	What time is normally best?
SECRETARY:	You could try around nine o'clock.

After all this said and done, you hang up, take another minute to write down when he'll be available. File the card somewhere. Set your mental alarm. And you may or may not remember to call him back at nine in the morning.

This entire exercise, collecting call-back information from secretaries, will take about a minute and a half. And worst of all, the information you collected is worthless.

In 1978, I spent one afternoon testing the "no call-back information principle." We called for several hours and every time a secretary would say that Mr. Jones was not in, I would ask her when he was expected in. I would note down that time. And then I would call back within five minutes of that time. If I couldn't place the call within the five minutes, I would just forget about it. In essence, what I was doing was developing a separate list of executives based on secretarial information. And obviously what I wanted to know was: Is this list any good?

When I tallied up my results, I found that I got much better results per unit of time invested by simply asking for Mr. Jones, and if he wasn't in or not available, going on to the next call. I concluded that by asking for call-back information, I was developing a list of the people who tended to be away from the office. Therefore, all time spent in developing that list was wasted. And all time spent calling it was wasted.

Here's how the conversation should have gone:

YOU: *Ring, ring*

SECRETARY: Mr. Jones's office.

YOU: Hi, is he in?

SECRETARY: He's not in right now. May I take a message.

YOU: No thanks. I'll call back. *Click. Dial tone.*

If you want to destroy your daytime rate, simply call and find out from secretaries when Mr. or Ms. Jones will be in. Now write the answer down. Spend more time organizing it. And spend still more time calling it back. This will cut a decent daytime call-back rate from forty or fifty calls per hour all the way down to twelve.

Don't Leave Messages

If you want to destroy your calling rate even further, leave messages with secretaries. That's good for an additional minute. Unless the boss knows you, he or she won't call back, so the time you're spending with the secretary is wasted. Don't do it.

HOW TO BYPASS OR HANDLE SECRETARIES

Surely secretaries are the bone in the throat of most salespeople. They are the lion at the door. The dog at the gate. If only you could get past that secretary and talk to Mr. or Ms. Jones, well, surely he or she would buy.

But there sits the secretary.

In some locations, Canada for one, small towns for another, the secretary is not a particular problem. But in the major metropolitan markets with their high-powered, big-budget executives, there are thousands of salespeople banging away at the phones and doors. Very literally, if salespeople could all get through and talk to the boss, he or she would be unable to do anything else. Therefore, a secretary is planted at the door with instructions to screen the calls.

You may wonder why I've included this section on secretaries in the section on how to make more calls. The reason should be obvious. Secretaries can waste a great amount of your time. Handling them correctly will enormously increase your number of calls and therefore your number of contacts.

A broad principle for dealing with secretaries is this: When the secretary tells you the boss is a pit, please believe him or her. A secretary knows the boss better than you.

Other methods of telephone marketing have recommended fairly brutal treatment for the secretary. A typical Old School conversation, using these methods, might go like this:

YOU: *Ring, ring.*

SECRETARY: Good morning. Mr. Jones's office.

YOU: Is he in?

SECRETARY: May I tell him who's calling?

YOU: It's Fred Smithers. I'd like to speak with him. Is he in?

SECRETARY: May I tell him what the call is about?

YOU: Yes, you can tell him it's Fred Smithers calling. I need to speak with him at once. Please connect me.

In other words, practitioners of this method try and intimidate the secretary and shove their way past. And it will work. However, if you are successful in getting through to Mr. or Ms. Jones, please remember you will be calling back again. Don't worry, the secretary will remember. And the hold button is a very long place to be.

A practitioner of this method can always get me to come to the

177

phone if he or she calls and treats my secretary this way. My secretary will tell me, "I've got another jerk." I will get on the phone and explain that the "shove your way in the door" tactic is gross and tell them if they wish to call back politely, no problem. They never do.

With this in mind, let's lay out six different methods for handling secretaries. I'm giving you these in order of preference. Please keep in mind that there is no way to tell which method will work best for which list in which city.

Method 1: Answer the secretary's questions first

There is an old saying in sales, "the one who asks the questions controls the conversation." This may be a holdover from the Old School, but it nevertheless remains true.

You can actually develop a method for handling the secretary based on this principle. The way most salespeople commonly call for the decision maker leaves the secretary in full control. The secretary asks all the questions: who you are, what company you're with, and what you want.

In Method 1, you take control by anticipating and answering all those questions first, and then by asking a question yourself, so you get some control.

Here is how this method might work:

YOU: *Ring, ring.*

SECRETARY: Good morning. Mr. Jones's office.

YOU: Good morning. This is Fred Smithers. I'm with the Acme Company. I need to speak with him about his money. Could you connect me please?

SECRETARY: (Uncertain) Just a moment. I'll see if he's in.

MR. JONES: Hello.

Now granted, this method does not work all the time. Its primary benefits to you, the salesperson, are that it does dislodge the secretary a bit from the control position, and it is very quick.

Remember, if your decision maker does not want to talk to you, you don't want to talk to him or her.

Obviously, the exact words that you use to tell the secretary what your call is about are critical. Remember, one primary function of a good secretary is to relay communication. Method 1 uses this function, and your objective is to get him or her to relay a message that will strike the decision maker as important enough or interesting enough to come to the phone.

In Financial Services, I have found the best word to use is "money." If your call has anything to do with saving, investing, speculating, or even buying anything, your best word is "money." Here's the message the secretary will relay to Mr. Jones:

SECRETARY: Hey, Fred! There is some guy on the phone from Acme Company. He said it's about your money.

Now Fred has got to be wondering, "What money?" His money? The company's money? His wife's money? What's going on? So he'll take the call to satisfy his curiosity. Always remember that curiosity is at least as powerful a motive for action as greed or interest.

If you can't use the word "money" when you tell the secretary what your call is about, simply experiment with different descriptions of what you want to talk to Mr. Jones about. Try and find a combination of words that will get you through. If you aren't getting through, keeping experimenting with a different message.

Here's a hint: Try the obvious.

If you're a commercial real estate agent: "It's about the lease on your building there at 404 Main Street."

If you sell seminars: "It's about a seminar that can help your salespeople find lots of new business."

If you sell cars: "It's about that old clunker you drive."

Method 2: Slide By

This is a technique that will work on many secretaries. The secretarial position is one with an enormously high turnover. Perhaps as many as thirty to forty percent of the nation's secretaries change jobs yearly. So your chances are pretty good that you'll speak with a secretary who is not certain you have the right to talk to Mr. Jones.

As you prepare to test out this method, I should warn you that there is a type of secretary we call the "office queen," although it naturally applies to both sexes. She is normally the secretary to a high-level executive, has been there since Year One, and may in fact be one of the most powerful people in a major corporation. Undoubtedly she lives there, and the slide by approach won't work with her. Further, if you try to slide by, she will sever your hand at the wrist, smile politely, and hand it back to you in a perfumed paper bag neatly wrapped.

With that warning in place, let's discuss how you can slide by many, if not most, secretaries. The steps in this method are:

1) Know the name of the person you wish to speak to.

2) Get the secretary's name from reception.

3) Slide by.

Here is how it works:

YOU:	*Ring, ring.*
RECEPTIONIST:	Good morning. Acme Company.
YOU:	Good morning. I need to speak to Mr. Jones's secretary. Could you tell me her name please?
RECEPTIONIST:	Beverly Smith.
YOU:	Would you connect me please?
RECEPTIONIST:	*Ring, ring.*
SECRETARY:	Good Morning. Mr. Jones's office.
YOU:	Hi, Bev! This is Fred. Is Ralph in?
SECRETARY:	(Feeling terror at the possibility of insulting a friend of the boss.) Just a moment please. *Ring, ring.*
MR. JONES:	Hello.

Method 3: **Pre-approach Phone Call**

Here is a theory for you. Behind the administrative screen of a well-defended list lies an undersolicited prospect. If you stop and think about it, you can see why. This executive has hired someone to screen his or her calls. Most calls, therefore, don't get through. The executive, then, does not receive his or her fair share of prospecting phone calls. Conclusion: If you can get hold of him or her, you might have a very good prospect.

So the name of the game becomes: Penetrate the screen.

The method I'm going to outline for you should not be used on routine lists. It is best on a well-defended list. For example, you may want to use it on a list of senior executives for the *Fortune* 500 companies in your city. Use it if you've already tried Method 1 or Method 2 and found that they didn't work.

Step 1 of the technique is a call in which you don't even try to speak to the boss. This is literally the pre-approach phone call. It corresponds to and serves the same purpose as a pre-approach letter. It paves the way. Here it goes:

YOU:	*Ring, ring.*
SECRETARY:	Good morning. Ms. Jones's office.
YOU:	Good morning. This is Fred Smithers with the Acme Company. Please tell Ms. Jones I'll be calling her this afternoon between two o'clock and three o'clock. It's about an important idea that can substantially cut her computer supply costs. Okay?
SECRETARY:	Very good. I'll tell her.
YOU:	By the way, who am I speaking with?
SECRETARY:	This is Beverly.
YOU:	Very good, Beverly. I'll give her a jingle this afternoon.

181

Write down the secretary's name. As a matter of fact, any time you get a secretary's name, write it down! And use it! Get the secretary on your side.

Step 2 of the technique is the follow-up phone call in which you do try to get through to the boss. Here you're going to capitalize on the fact that you know the secretary's name and that the boss is expecting the call. Here's how it goes:

YOU: *Ring, ring.*

SECRETARY: Good afternoon, Ms. Jones's office.

YOU: Hi, Beverly, it's Fred over here at Acme. She should be expecting my call. Would you connect me please?

This method was tested out by a stockbroker operating in one of the most highly resistant markets there is: New York City. She found that the time spent calling in the morning plus the time spent calling in the afternoon added up to better results than just calling and asking for Ms. Jones.

Remember, always evaluate any campaign or technique by results per units of time. Here the key factor to evaluate is the number of qualified prospects per unit of time and percentage of those which are cherries.

Method 4: The Message Campaign

There are some lists that are impossible to prospect by phone. Or should we say, are impossible to prospect by phone without the use of the message campaign.

Take doctors, for instance. Cold calling doctors is like calling nowhere. They are always "with a patient." In fact, a new machine has been invented that only says, "Doctor's office" and "He's/She's with a patient." Other lists are nearly as impossible to call because the people have jobs that take them away from the office. You'll seldom reach sales managers or salespeople who work out of the office.

The solution is the message campaign. In a message campaign, you call up and very quickly leave a message with the secretary or receptionist. If the prospect is interested, he or she will return the call.

Now this brings up a very important question. Earlier, I told you "Don't Leave Messages." And yet here I am telling you to leave messages.

What I'm really telling you is don't mix the two procedures. Either go after your decision maker and get him or forget him. Or, call up and *only* leave a message and *don't* try to get him to the phone.

As a broad rule of thumb, hang up on answering machines. A possible exception is doctor's machines. If you leave the message, "It's about your money," I guarantee you will get a return call.

Properly done, there is an actual rhythm to cold calling. It seems to work best with a single limited objective. Where your approach has got many legs to it, you will feel, at the end of an hour or two, utterly splattered and pulled apart. Your rhythm will be broken and it will cost you dearly in terms of number of calls that you make. However, see how the message campaign works with a single objective when calling a doctor.

YOU:	*Ring, ring.*
RECEPTIONIST:	Doctor Jones's office.
YOU:	Good morning. I have an important message for Dr. Jones. Will you write it down?
RECEPTIONIST:	Yes, I will.
YOU:	My name is Fred Smithers, I work at Acme Company. My phone number is 665–4821. The message is: It's about your car. Did you get that?
RECEPTIONIST:	Yes, I did.
YOU:	Thankyouverymuch. *Click. Dial tone.*

There is a principle involved here. The principle is, don't tell everything in your message. Secondly, keep your message as short as possible. Seven words or less is the rule of thumb. Our message

—"It's about your car"—might certainly get the doctor to call back. If you're selling a financial product or service, don't name it. Name a benefit. Or better yet simply paint a mystery picture. Possibly the most effective message campaign I ever developed was for a tax shelter product. One afternoon in Phoenix, we called doctors, and our message was simply, "It's about a portable tax shelter."

Within minutes, the phone began ringing with doctors calling in to find out what on earth a portable tax shelter was. And that, of course, was the idea.

Method 5: Ask 'em a question they can't answer

This is a method designed for a well-defended, but reachable, list. It's not for a list like doctors, who are not reachable.

In this method, you are simply going to act as if the secretary is the decision maker and then ask the secretary a question that he or she can't answer. If possible, you'll also appeal to the secretary's own self-interest. The minute his or her feet are held slightly to the fire, if Ms. Jones is in at all, the secretary will probably transfer you.

I used this technique very effectively in a campaign I designed for a group of Western Union salespeople. Our objective was to contact the comptrollers of *Fortune* 500 companies and get them involved in bulk use of Mailgrams for credit collection purposes.

Our call to the secretary went like this:

YOU: *Ring, ring.*

SECRETARY: Good morning. Ms. Jones's office.

YOU: Good morning. This is Fred Smithers with Western Union. Are you Ms. Jones's secretary?

SECRETARY: Yes I am. My name is Frank.

YOU: Very good, Frank. I'm calling because Western Union has developed a new method to help with your credit collection. Tell me, what percentage of your accounts go delinquent after ninety days?

184

SECRETARY: Ummmmmm. I'm not sure. Perhaps you'd better speak with Ms. Jones.

The key to this method, of course, is to ask a question the secretary can't answer. It should be a question that only the boss can answer.

Here is an example, using the same principle, for an insurance agent to call pension and profit-sharing plans. Note the way I have appealed to the secretary's self-interest. I have underlined appropriate passages.

TO SECRETARY: Good morning/afternoon. This is _____ with _____. Are you M/M _____'s secretary? And who am I speaking with? Great! Perhaps you can help me. I would like to send M/M _____ some information on our pension fund management program that can very possibly increase the <u>amount of money (COMPANY NAME) employees will get at retirement.</u> But I need to know exactly what kind of plan you have now. Is it a qualified corporate, HR-10, Super IRA or PEDC? (RESPONSE) Perhaps M/M _____ has that info on the tip of (HIS/HER) tongue. Could you connect me please?

Method 6: The Mad Dog Method

Strictly speaking, the method I outline here will not help you increase your number of calls. Rather, it is a humorous, and highly effective, example of a way to get through to a single decision maker that you want *very badly* to reach. The method was first used by a broker whose nickname is Mad Dog Mike. Although now a branch manager, he first earned fame as one of the best cold-calling brokers around.

As Mike told the story to me, he read one day that a very wealthy man in Northern California had sold a big piece of property for a substantial amount of money. Mike immediately called up and encountered the classic office queen. We'll call her Mildred. When Mike tried to get through to Mr. Jones, Mildred explained to him, "Mike, I assure you, he is very well taken care of. He has several brokers and does not require your services."

So over the next few days, Mike tried all the standard ploys to get through to Mr. Jones. He called at one minute before nine, at one minute after twelve, at ten in the morning, late in the afternoon, and so on, thinking Mildred would be on break. Nothing worked. She seemed to live there.

So one day, Mike called Mildred up and he said to her, "Mildred, I just want to let you know that I'm now setting my clock."

MILDRED: You're doing what?

MIKE: I'm setting my clock. I'm setting it to go off at exactly nine o'clock and every morning when it goes off at nine o'clock I'm going to call you. And Mildred, I'm going to call you every day until I die.

Mike began doing it. After a while, word got out in the office, and each morning at nine, the office would gather around Mike's desk for his morning call. A typical call would go like this:

MIKE: *Ring, ring.*

MILDRED: Good morning, Mr. Jones's office.

MIKE: Good morning Mildred, it's me.

MILDRED: Mike!

MIKE: Is he in?

MILDRED: You know you can't talk to him.

MIKE: Thankyouverymuch. Call you tomorrow. *Click. Dial tone.*

This went on for several weeks. Finally one morning Mildred said, "I can't stand it anymore. I'm going to let you talk to him."

So, Mike at long last got on the phone with Mr. Jones. Here's what he said.

186

MIKE: Good morning. As I'm sure Mildred has told you, I've been calling quite a bit lately, and I just want to let you know, if you have any questions at all you can give me a call, okay?

MR. JONES: Ah, okay.

MIKE: Very good. Thankyouverymuch. *Click. Dial tone.*

Shortly thereafter, Mr. Jones called back.

"Okay," he said, "You've got my attention." And Mike got the account.

KEEPING TRACK

When I started telephone sales as a part-time job in 1974, I found out very quickly the truth of the "sales is a numbers game" principle. Very possibly, my first inkling that the Old School was full of it was my observation that the more calls I could make the better results I would get. Right there, if I had really examined it, I would have seen the utter nonsense of the "Don't-believe-the-prospect-until-he-has-said-no-forty-two-times" school. The full insight was to come some years later.

What did come very clear to me was the importance of setting goals for number of calls *on an hourly basis* and then tracking my goal by the hour. I found that any hour I didn't make my "number of dials" goal was an hour in which I didn't make my sales goals. I finally got to the point where the number of calls was far more important than pursuing a long-winded prospect who might, or most likely would not, buy. On the next two pages, I am reproducing two charts that may help you keep track.

Chart 1 is designed to be used for each day's calling. Chart 2 is to summarize weekly results. At the end of a day, simply tally up your results from Chart 1 and write them down on Chart 2. Managers would do well to use Chart 2. Your salespeople should fill out Chart 1 and then turn it in to you. You inspect it and comment on it and then return it to them. At the end of the week, you file Chart 2 in their folder. This gives you a running record of

CALL SHEET

Name _____

_____   _____   _____
Time Start   **Time Done**   **Day and Date**

_____   _____   _____
                                Results: **Dials Per Hour**   **Prospects**

PROSPECT LISTS CALLED: _____

CALLED ON (_____**)**
                        Script

																				Time
1	2	3	4	5	6	7	8	9	10	11	12	13	14	15	16	17	18	19	20	___
21	22	23	24	25	26	27	28	29	30	31	32	33	34	35	36	37	38	39	40	___
41	42	43	44	45	46	47	48	49	50	51	52	53	54	55	56	57	58	59	60	___
61	62	63	64	65	66	67	68	69	70	71	72	73	74	75	76	77	78	79	80	___
81	82	83	84	85	86	87	88	89	90	91	92	93	94	95	96	97	98	99	100	___

CODE: / = That number DIALED
            X = CONTACT with decision maker
            O = CHERRY
            + = GREEN CHERRY

CALLBACKS

ONLY RECORD CONTACTS:

1	2	3	4	5	6	7	8	9	10	11	12	13	14	15	16	17	18	19	20
21	22	23	24	25	26	27	28	29	30	31	32	33	34	35	36	37	38	39	40

CODE: / = CONTACTED
            O = Appointment Set
            ⟩ = New Account Opened

CALLBACK RESULTS: _____   _____   _____
                        Contacts   **Appts. Set**   **New Account**

Chart 1

how each salesperson does week to week. If you do this, you will have gone a long way to developing an early warning system of impending disaster. When something goes wrong, calls will drop.

Here's how to use your Call Sheet:

Every time you make a dial, put a slash mark through the number. If the call turns into a "contact with decision maker," put

DAILY / WEEKLY REPORT

DAY	DIALS	CONTACTS	CHERRIES	GREEN CHERRIES
MON				
TUE				
WED				
THU				
FRI				
SAT				

TOTAL DIALS	CONTACTS	CHERRIES	GREENIES

Chart 2

another mark so now you have an X. If the contact then turns into a cherry, draw a circle around it. If it's a green cherry, make a cross next to it. When you get to the end of a row of numbers, jot down the time. Your objective is twenty calls in twenty minutes. Here is a sample row of numbers with the codes explained.

/ / X Ⓧ ✝ 6 7 8 9 10 11 12 13 14 15 16 17 18 19 20 _ _ _

The first call was busy. So it's just marked as a dial.
The second call was disconnected. It's also marked as a dial.
The third call was a jerk, but we did talk to a decision maker.
The fourth call is a cherry. It's marked with a circled X.
The fifth call is a green cherry. He's marked with a cross.

189

HOW TO USE "NUMBER OF CALLS"

The very first thing to check when you are not getting three cherries per hour is the number of calls. If you are keeping your Call Sheet, just glance over at it. If you are dialing more than forty calls an hour and not getting three cherries an hour, the problem lies elsewhere.

11

Breakout: Putting It All Together

The first part of this chapter is really for salespeople only. You managers have an entire chapter coming up just for you, and I want to talk for a moment to salespeople about getting a job in sales. A job is, after all, the first thing a salesperson needs if he or she is, as the title of this chapter suggests, going to "put it together." So you managers just go ahead and skip down to the next section titled "The Breakout Plan."

FOR SALESPEOPLE ONLY

I frequently run into salespeople who ask me whether they should go and work for this company or that company. Over the years, I have developed a pretty good understanding that it really doesn't matter so much whether you go to work for one or the other as long as you're working for a decent, honest company with a good product or service to sell. What matters a great deal more is which *manager* you work for. Whether he or she is called a branch manager, general agent, broker, sales manager, or supreme leader, your manager will be the most important person in your life for the next two years. (If you can survive the first two years, you can survive as long as you choose. By then, you're a professional.) I know branch managers in the brokerage industry who have almost never lost an account executive due to failure. And rarely have they ever lost one to a head hunter from another firm. These managers train, manage, and motivate their sales crew to become winners.

So if you are out looking for a sales job, don't take the first offer you get. Here are some things to look for in a manager.

1) Can the manager see into the sales room from his or her office?

This may sound like an odd requirement. However, I've seen too many managers who get behind closed doors, crunch their numbers, and never become really involved with the day-to-day activities of their sales force. They are protected by iron maiden secretaries, intimidating offices, throne-like desks, and while they may be very successful as sales managers, it's more likely they inherited an office with big hitters rather than grew their big hitters from scratch. You want an office where the manager is *involved*.

2) Find out what the manager's turnover is.

Ask the manager, "If you hired ten people a year ago, how many of them are with you today?" And then ask, "How much money are the ones who are still with you today making?" And finally, "Do you mind if I talk to two or three of your one-year salespeople?"

In talking with those salespeople, find out what you get in the way of additional training. Does the sales manager himself or herself ever go and make sales calls? And of course find out how much money the one-year survivor is making by asking him or her as well as the manager.

3) Ask what the manager expects in the way of hours.

If you get a typical forty-hour-a-week answer, know that you are probably doomed to failure in that office. It takes a substantial commitment to get a new sales career off the ground, and if anybody tells you you can do it by seeing only the old customers in a territory, you can figure at best you're good for $20,000 or $22,000 a year. If you exceed that, they may cut your territory and you'll starve to death.

4) Find out if you can do the work.

If possible, ask to go out on a sales call with one of the one-year survivors and with someone who is established in the business. See if it's the kind of work you can do. I can tell you this for certain. If you don't like the work, or if you don't like the people to whom you sell, you are dooming yourself to a life of misery and frustration. What could be worse than getting up in the morning to go sell something you don't like to people you despise?

THE BREAKOUT PLAN

Some time ago, I received a letter from a branch manager in the securities industry. He told me that six of his brokers had been following my system for a couple of months, were putting in seven hours a week, ten hours a week, and they were getting really discouraged. These six brokers had, in two months, opened only thirty-five new accounts. That's an average of three per month per broker, which is certainly a free ticket to the food stamp line.

My advice to him was to keep the brokers' feet to the fire because I could see an all-too-familiar pattern unfolding. The pattern is: Salesperson starts calling; salesperson gets middling or poor results, maybe even after hanging in there for a couple of months. Salesperson gives up. In reality, "the give up" almost always occurs at about the five-yard line, when you're almost there.

In the third month, this group of brokers "broke loose." My friend called to tell me that one of them opened seven accounts in a week. The next week, another followed with five accounts. The others bounced out of the pits as well. And once again, I saw this almost magical phenomenon I have come to call Breakout occur. And occur it does . . . especially if you don't give up at the five-yard line. Breakout is a sudden explosion of new business. Why does it occur? Let's compare the prospecting procedure we've developed with a pipeline. Pump oil in one end of a pipeline, and after a while it will come out the other end. Even pumping hard and fast, at first you'll only get a trickle *and then suddenly*

193

a torrent. Just like a real pipeline, if you stuff in lists, dials, cherries, second calls, appointments, closing calls, and closes, out the other end will come new accounts and commissions. And the new accounts seem to first trickle out, and then BANG! You've got Breakout.

In some industries, this pipeline is short, perhaps a matter of days. In other industries, like commercial real estate, it may be years. But whatever industry you're in, *it will occur.*

The Breakout Plan, then, is to stuff the pipeline with lots of prospects *and keep doing it for a period of weeks or months* until you get the explosion—Breakout!

CREATING BREAKOUT

Let's first talk work habits.

Two hours of calling this week, four next week, a down week, and one hour the next week will create NOTHING. Just like an airplane taking off, a certain minimum amount of energy is required to create Breakout. Less than that gets a pitiful dribble. And that leads you to believe the system is a failure. It isn't. It just doesn't have enough energy.

The energy for a prospecting system comes from hours spent making forty to sixty dials of the phone an hour. How many hours a week? Somewhere between seven on a low end and fourteen tops. I'm talking about hours spent making *first calls.* These hours do not include hours spent doing second calls, appointments, and so forth. We stuff the pipeline first with hours and dials. These generate cherries, which in turn create second calls. And so on through the pipeline. But with no hours and dials, there is nothing going in. *And therefore, nothing will come out.*

Why seven hours? Because I have never seen anyone sustain a commitment when they started with less than that. Apparently, less than that produces so few prospects that the salesperson loses interest. But look at this: If you do seven hours a week for twelve weeks, if you average three cherries per hour, in twelve weeks you'll have 252 prospects in various stages of closing. You tell me that won't create a Breakout!

When should you do your seven hours?

If your prospects can be reached night or day, do one hour a day *every day* and then one evening of two hours.

If your prospects can only be reached during the day, do an hour every morning, and then spend two hours late one afternoon (after the secretary has gone home!). And keep doing this for at least twelve weeks. Unless you are in a field like commercial real estate, you'll get Breakout in twelve weeks.

So make the commitment now: a minimum of seven hours a week for twelve *consecutive* weeks. If you miss a week, you owe next week. This is a commitment with yourself to create your future. If you're brand new in business, just double everything and keep on that schedule until you cannot possibly see everyone you have developed as a cherry.

The One-Hour Test

Here's how you start. Grab a list. Any list. Write a script. As you write it, try and stay within one of the forms we've covered, but some script is better than none. Just make sure it's in writing.

Call the list using the script. Stick to that script for an hour. If it's obvious in midstream that it needs changing, make the changes in writing. Then start a new one-hour test. The chances are that you will not get your three cherries an hour right off the bat. So what? Rome wasn't built in a day.

Now do another one-hour test. If you didn't get your three cherries an hour in your first hour, work on your script. Or work on your number of dials per hour. Early on, you'll want to concentrate on your wording, your dials, and your list.

Upgrade Your List

Chances are excellent that the first list you grabbed for your first test is not the best list you could use. The important thing is this: The *FIRST THING* you do is call. THEN organize your lists. *Start calling first.* Keep calling, and as you do, upgrade your list and work on and improve your script. Frankly, I have seen too many salespeople in too many industries spend too much time on organization and never make the first dial. If the only thing in sight is

195

the White Pages, grab 'em and start. And then, in your *nonoptimum calling time,* get to the library or wherever and start putting together your own specialized lists.

The First Call

Without a doubt, the hardest call to make is the first one. As you sit in front of your telephone with palms sweating and throat dry, you just know this isn't for you.

Since this system *is different* from whatever you've done in the past, I know that you will feel uncomfortable. You definitely felt uncomfortable the first time you passed an eighteen-wheeler after getting your driver's license. You undoubtedly felt uncomfortable the first time you made a sales presentation. And you were certainly uncomfortable the first time you ever stood up in front of a group of people to give a talk.

So what else is new? You'll feel uncomfortable the first time you do *anything* new, and you certainly should not evaluate whether you're going to do something on the basis of whether it feels comfortable or not. Evaluate it on whether it makes sense to you or not, and then know that because it is new, you will feel uncomfortable. So what?

You didn't let that stop you from passing the truck, making the sales presentation, or standing up in front of a group. Don't let it stop you now.

Keeping Going

It's very probable that you may be the only one in your company or group that is studying this system and implementing it. You may or may not get much help from your manager, and you probably won't get much help from the other salespeople in your group.

So you'll need some techniques to keep your morale up and keep the ball rolling long enough for you to hit Breakout.

So here are some suggestions:

1) MONITOR YOUR PROGRESS BY THE HOUR ON FIRST CALLS.

I've already given you a sample call sheet. This call sheet is built around the 20/20 plan. Twenty dials in twenty minutes. Yes, I know I've said forty dials an hour, but let's make it interesting and shoot for sixty. By putting your attention on number of dials, you won't have time to think about whether you're succeeding with this person or that person. And that's the whole point.

Don't worry about how you're doing while you're doing it. That's why you're keeping records so that later you can step back and look at them. If you're doing well, you'll feel good. If it's not working for you, you can begin to use the numbers you generate in order to figure out why.

2) KEEP TO YOURSELF.

This is a note of warning. I have observed in many cases that a group of salespeople will turn, almost savagely, on someone who threatens to move out of it and succeed on a grand scale. By succeeding, you'll be giving a slap in the face to those who have banded together at a low level of sales. And they don't like that. I have seen friendships dissolve, vicious rumors started, and things disappear off the desks of salespeople on the move. For whatever reason, the group you're in probably won't like it—and you—if you succeed.

So keep to yourself whatever plans you have for success. Don't make a big thing about your plans. Just quietly set out on your seven- or fourteen-hour-a-week plan, test your list, and so on. As success comes your way—which it must if you do all of the things outlined in this book—you might elect to share what you've been doing with a few select associates. But select them with care. If this sounds harsh, it's only because I have observed too many good people damaged by those who would remain in the mire of mediocrity.

3) STICK TO YOUR PLAN FOR AT LEAST TWELVE WEEKS.

It's too easy to quit at the five-yard line. Don't do it!

IF IT'S NOT WORKING

Dealing with ever-changing human beings as we do, there is certainly no guarantee that your first, or even tenth approach is going to work and deliver the kind of results that you want. Hopefully, by now you understand that I have not given you a ticket to success but rather the tools to build your own railroad. So in this section, let's pull it all together and learn how to use these tools to fix it if it's broke. Remember, however, *if it ain't broke, don't fix it.*

First, let's review the elements we have gone over to create a campaign. Then we'll look at them again, from a different point of view, and see how to use them to unstick a campaign that's stuck.

The Variables

Let's define the term "variable" as anything over which the individual or company has control that can *change the outcome* of a prospecting or direct marketing campaign.

In prospecting or direct marketing, you will need to learn to think with variables. We have spent virtually the entire book discussing them in detail. These variables are the analytical tools you'll use the most. You use them to plan a campaign to begin with, to correct it when it fails, and to lock it in when it succeeds.

Perhaps the concept can be grasped best from a story about a young man who didn't get the idea at all. Some years ago, I had trained a stockbroker in Los Angeles (whom I'll call Ernie). When Ernie went through my initial seminar, he seemed to be doing fine. He was bright, aggressive, had a good voice, and in short, seemed to have everything going for him that it would take to succeed. At least, he had everything going that would help him succeed in opening new accounts. How he would manage those accounts, well, that can sometimes be a different story.

About two weeks after I first trained Ernie, I bumped into him in downtown Los Angeles. I remember our conversation well:

BILL: Ernie, how are you doing?

ERNIE: No good.

BILL: What's happening?

ERNIE: Not much. I'm the only member of our class who hasn't sold anything yet.

BILL: Hummmm. Sounds bad. Tell me, what's going on?

ERNIE: They are just not buying.

BILL: Who's not buying?

ERNIE: The people I'm calling.

BILL: Who are you calling?

ERNIE: The Beverly Hills Yellow Pages.

BILL: Hummm. How long have you been calling the Beverly Hills Yellow Pages?

ERNIE: For the last two weeks. It's terrible. I can't even get anyone to talk to me.

BILL: You doughball. You sat through my seminar, and then you've been calling the same list of jerks for an entire two weeks. Come with me.

I literally grabbed Ernie by the ear, hauled him into the office, and grabbed the North Long Beach Yellow Pages.

"Here," I said. "Call these. At least in North Long Beach, the business people are not in hock up to their eyebrows to the landlords. Plus you should know that practically any stockbroker, insurance agent, light-bulb salesperson, and so on, is going to call the poor slobs in Beverly Hills because they are the first and most obvious people that have some money. Their resistance is unbelievable. Throw them away."

Within an hour, Ernie had found a prospect who three days later bought $70,000 worth of bonds. As he reported to me, the difference in calling North Long Beach versus calling Beverly Hills was like calling a place where there were people versus some uninhabited wasteland of robots that answered the phone and were programmed to act like jerks.

So what was it Ernie missed? He missed the fact that *you can change your results by changing a variable!* I changed his list, and he went from poor results to excellent results!

A variable is something you control that affects the results of what you do. With that idea firmly in mind, let's take a brief look

199

at the variables of a telephone prospecting campaign. We've studied them in detail. Now let's look at them in summary form. They are:

1) YOUR BASIC PHILOSOPHY

You have three choices. The Old School, with its philosophy of overcoming resistance and persisting through innumerable consecutive turndowns. Or the New School, which believes there are enough prospects in most any market area who are interested and qualified now to make a search for those worthwhile and ignore the rest until later. Or you can place yourself somewhere in between. You will need to work out for yourself what you believe. I trust you do see the extent to which this can affect results.

2) WHO YOU CALL

This is your list of prospective customers. Some of your most dramatic changes in results will come from a change in your list.

3) WHAT YOU SAY

This is your sales message, your actual words. It corresponds in importance and results to the text of a direct-mail letter. Change your words and I guarantee you'll change results, sometimes for the better, sometimes for the worse.

4) HOW MANY YOU CALL PER UNIT OF TIME

This variable is obviously related to the length of your message. If you are making a long-winded call, you can't make very many of them. This is not necessarily to say that you shouldn't make long-winded calls, but it is to say that your ability to do so effectively is governed by the quality of your list. If your list is just an average list, you really have to move through it quickly to find those cherries., But if it is a superb, well-researched list, not only can you spend a bit more time but you can achieve more per call.

5) HOW YOU SOUND

In telephone marketing, where "sound" and "words" are the only means of communication, "sound" is certainly very important.

6) WHEN YOU CALL

This refers to the time of day you call a particular list. If you follow the approach to list development that I recommend, you'll find that the better job you do defining your list, the more likely you are to find one or several times during the week when that list yields best results.

Let's take an example. Let's say you have developed a list of real estate brokers who earn more than $50,000 per year. I guarantee you that the people on this list, who are united both by occupation and earnings, will also have certain work patterns in common. You can count on great difficulty reaching them on Tuesday mornings, which is the time most residential agents view property for sale. So you might find that the only time to call this list on Tuesdays is very early in the morning at their offices before they leave for the day. You would discover this through test and experience.

Using Variables to Create a Campaign

1) Decide which basic philosophy to try or test.

2) Select a list.

3) Develop a message.

4) Determine a particular time of day to call.

5) Set a goal for a certain number of dials an hour.

6) Lock in a professional sound.

7) Roll it out.

If you can't get three cherries an hour, change a variable. If, after several attempts to bring up to three, go through the Basic Skills Checklist below. If you still can't get your three an hour, throw away your list if its the worst list you have. Always weed your lists from the bottom up.

Basic Skills Checklist

If you can't make it work, take each of the points below and do whatever it takes to turn a "No" answer into a "Yes."

1) ARE YOU ABLE TO GET THROUGH TO PEOPLE AND TALK TO THEM?

I've seen some people bog down right here. They've got a list that is unreachable. If you can't reach the people on your list, follow the steps below. If these don't work, try a direct-mail campaign to the list. It's for certain no one else is calling the list either.

A) Restudy that portion of your script that deals with secretaries. If you've been trying a standard method, switch and try the pre-approach phone call, message campaign, or buddy-buddy.

B) If none of these works, try simply asking for the direct extension number when the secretary says, "He's not interested," "not in," or whatever. Say, "That's fine. I'll call him first thing in the morning. What's his direct extension number?" And then try the prospect early in the morning.

C) Try alternate times during the day to get through.

2) DO YOU HAVE A WRITTEN SCRIPT?

Please note that the question is not: Do you have a script? If you are making repetitive calls, you will have. But have you written it down? If you have not written it down, changes will begin creeping into your call, and before long, what may have started out as a tight, disciplined one-minute phone call is now a blubbering, bloated call. If it's not written down, write it down.

3) ARE YOU ASKING FOR "JUST THE RIGHT AMOUNT OF COMMITMENT" ON YOUR SCRIPT?

Here we get into the difference between going for an appointment on the first call and going for a qualified prospect. It may be that you are asking too much. If you are, redo your script and use a multicall approach as outlined in chapters 4 and 5.

4) DOES YOUR SCRIPT OFFER A BENEFIT?

I can't tell you how many scripts I've heard that make absolutely no offer at all to their prospects. People want a benefit! If they are going to give you some time or commitment, you've got to give them something. Give them a benefit.

5) DOES YOUR SCRIPT OFFER THE *RIGHT* BENEFIT?

If your script does offer a benefit and if you're finding people are not interested in it, switch the benefit. There is no way to know on any one product which benefit is most likely to attract and hold immediate attention. So try several.

6) ARE YOU STICKING TO THE SCRIPT?

Or are you getting off the script so much you might as well not have it? If you have made a long-winded first call, you can certainly expect that you will have difficulty making that second call. So make certain that first call is less than a minute and a half long.

7) DO YOU QUALIFY FOR MONEY NOW?

One of the first things people drop out of their first call is the "money question." For whatever reason, people are shy or embarrassed about qualifying for money. You have to do it. If you don't do it, you're going to fill up your call-back file with pits and green cherries. Nothing against the poor, and quite frankly the poor may be your market, but they at least have to have enough money to buy your product. So if they don't have it, you don't want to talk to them.

8) ARE YOU MAKING AT LEAST FORTY DIALS OF THE PHONE AN HOUR?

An important thing to understand here is that if you're getting three cherries an hour you're doing it right. Sometimes you might make fewer calls than that and have lots of prospects. No problem. If you're getting three an hour you're doing it right. But if you're not getting three an hour and are making fewer than forty calls an hour, that ain't right. Press for dials. Implement the 20/20 plan.

9) DO YOU SOUND GOOD?

If the answer to this is yes, great! But you should go at least a step further and check these separate points of your sound:

- Do you sound sour, just as if you've been sucking a lemon?
- Is your inflection such that you sound uncertain and hesitant?

203

- Are you talking faster than your prospect?
- Are you talking more slowly than your prospect?
- Do you sound bored?
- Does your presentation sound canned?

To get an objective opinion, tape record your calls and play them for someone you trust. You might even play them for people not in sales at all and ask them what they think. Remember, most of these problems can be cured simply by rehearsal.

If you're unable to handle these problems on your own, I recommend very strongly that you take some voice lessons. I would actually call the drama department of a local school, college, or university. Get a good drama coach. Speech therapists are for those with severe handicaps. In the late 1960's, I took a few lessons from a drama coach to help me overcome some of the heavier sounds in my Southern accent. I still have parts of it, but it was so heavy that people would ask me, "What part of the South are you from?" That got very old; and as a professional speaker, I did not want people sitting there trying to figure out where I was from but instead wanted them to listen to what I was saying. The drama coach cured it in no time.

10) ARE YOU USING A GOOD LIST?

The only way to know if your list is good or bad is to isolate it as a variable. First, be sure that you have a good script for it, that you're making enough calls to it, that you sound good, and are calling and can get through. If you're getting two cherries an hour, you won't throw the list out. You'll work to replace it. Go spend more time on list development while keeping your calling campaign going. As soon as you've developed a list that can produce three cherries an hour, package up the one that will do two an hour and shoot it over to your competitor.

11) ARE YOU SETTING APPOINTMENTS ON YOUR SECOND CALL?

You should be getting forty to fifty percent of your cherries to set appointments with you. If not, check the following points:

- Are you calling back within five business days?

- Are you mutilating your material?

- Are you using your bypass principle as the introduction to your second call?

- Have you even written a second call script?

- Does it contain an ABC close, and is the benefit in the close an actual benefit or is it just a feature?

- Are you setting your appointments as close as possible to right now?

- If they are set more than five business days away, do you confirm each appointment in writing and then with a phone call the day before?

THE SALE BEGINS WHEN THE SALESPERSON SAYS "YES"

Elmer Letterman wrote one of the classics of the Old School. It's called *The Sale Begins When the Customer Says No.* If you have followed me this far, you know what I think of this idea. But the question Letterman answered his way in his book is a valid question: Where does the sale begin?

If you have fully understood prospecting *primarily as an act of discarding,* then you know the answer intuitively. The sale begins when you have attempted to discard and cannot. To put it another way, the sale begins when you, the salesperson, say, "Yes, you're worth spending my selling time with." This will only exist when the prospect has the interest, has the money, and has the capability to buy NOW. You then switch from prospecting mode to selling mode.

As I mentioned earlier, this switch from prospecting mode to selling mode can easily occur after your self-introduction. But it may not occur until after several in-person meetings. While you're prospecting, you're asking in all their dozens of forms the three basic prospecting questions: Are you interested enough? Can you afford it? Can you buy it? When you have answered those questions with a YES, you can start to sell the product.

What is Selling?

Let's define selling as showing your product or service to qualified prospects in such a way that you increase their desire for it to the point they want it badly enough to part with their money.

Quite obviously, there must then be some selling skills very different from the prospecting skills which have been the subject of this book. Among them are:

- Interviewing Skills. (Some trainers use the phrase "probing skills," but I reject that on personal grounds because I don't like to be "probed." And I don't think anyone else does either.) As a professional salesperson, you will need to interview your prospects to find out exactly which of your products or services they should buy first.

- Personal Presentation Skills. By this I mean your dress, style, and personal mannerisms, which can go a long way toward making —or blowing—a sale.

- People Watching Skills. These are skills you learn by calling or seeing in person *hundreds or thousands of people.* When I'm talking with someone by phone, I can see them. And I know when to close for the order.

- Product Presentation Skills. These are the skills you use to further increase interest and involvement. Most specifically, you'll want to concentrate on presenting the benefits of your product or service that most closely align with the prospect's goals.

- Closing Skills. These are the skills that enable the salesperson to get the prospect to make up his or her mind. Very literally, the word "close" means "to bring to a conclusion." It does not mean "sell" or "cause to buy." After you have done your very best in your presentation, you want the prospect to make up his or her mind. One way or the other. It's not the word "no" that kills off countless thousands or millions of salespeople. It's "Maybe." Closing skills enable you to convert some of the "Maybes" into "YES" and the rest into "No." No more "Maybe."

- Objection Handling Skills. Once you have decided that someone is a qualified prospect, you are no longer trying to discard them as you do when you prospect. Your entire frame of mind changes to one of "keep 'em." So you will need to answer objections in order to keep the sale going. In prospecting, when someone tells you, "I'm not interested," with the exceptions already noted, you let them go. But in selling, when they say, "I don't think I'm interested now," you don't just get up and leave. You find out why, attempt to handle the problem, and thereby rekindle interest, and your sale.

In the very back of this book is a page I've titled "For Further Improvement in Prospecting and Sales." I have recommended the best book on sales I know and the best set of tapes on closing. These can help you with your selling skills, or at least tide you over until I write my next book.

SOME FINAL THOUGHTS

Well, I've given it my best shot. If you want, you can go on and read the last chapter, "For Managers Only." You might learn a thing or two if you're just in sales itself. You might even decide that management is a place you'd like to be.

I would like to say this as a final observation. This system is definitely designed to generate too many prospects. Here's why. There are only three possibilities regarding the number of prospects:

1) You can have too many.

2) You can have too few.

3) You can have just the right number.

Needless to say, you'll never have just the right number. It's not going to happen. Having too few prospects is starvation for a salesperson. So my program is designed to generate too many. If the number you're generating literally overwhelms you, rejoice. But don't cut back on the number of hours you're calling. Instead, you may want to increase the qualification level. If you're an insurance salesman, instead of qualifying for ability to handle a $100 a month premium, go for $200. Since all you have is your time, ultimately, the only way to make more money is to spend it better. And for a salesperson that means spending it, first with more prospects and, second, spending it with more highly qualified prospects. Otherwise, you'll top out before you get rich. And after all, isn't getting rich why we all came into this business?

So, as we say on my end, Thankyouverymuch for reading this book. I hope you enjoyed it. I hope you use it. *Click. Dial Tone.*

12

For Managers Only
(Or How To Work Some Magic
with Your Sales Force)

In this chapter I am going to go over some ways a manager can help salespeople. As a salesperson, you can quite obviously learn something from this chapter. But it is designed primarily for the manager.

Most of the following techniques evolved in the two years before I started Telephone Marketing, Inc. This was my own training ground. It all started while I was sitting in my car in a four-and-a-half-hour gas line during the second Arab oil boycott.

At the time, I was the editor of a small magazine that catered to the restaurant trade. We were so undercapitalized that in order to pay the printing bill, we literally had to collect the money for our advertising in advance.

Now I don't know if you know much about restaurant owners, but they are an odd lot at best. Most of them are broke, and the only time they are around to talk to is during their lunch or dinner. But then they've got customers and problems in the kitchen, and so forth. So to sell our ads and get our money, we had to grab the owners during lunch or dinner and sit 'em down. Then we at least had a chance to sell and get the check.

When the oil boycott began, we were in deep trouble and knew it. At that time in Los Angeles, you could only get gas every other day. And then you had to wait for hours. Given the driving distances in Los Angeles, if you had one of the big old clunkers, a tank of gas could be gone in an afternoon.

So there I was, just off Franklin Avenue, sitting in a gas line and watching my job swirl down the drain. As I sat there, the question in my mind was, "There's got to be something else I can do." And then, like some kind of flash, I had it! I saw the gasoline problems

208

getting worse. I saw prices going out of sight. And somehow I saw a lot of changes were in store for marketing and sales.

Within a very few days I had decided it was time for a change for me. At that time, I didn't see my writing career was going anywhere. To be sure, I had been able to survive, but I spent more time writing about people making money and enjoying money than I did making it myself.

So I quit my job at the magazine, pulled out the classified ads of the Los Angeles *Times,* and got a job in telephone sales. And what I know today about managing and training large numbers of telephone salespeople really began with the first job I took.

In the pages that follow, I'm going to share with you some of the ideas that enabled me to go from nowhere to a position of considerable influence in several industries. First, of course, I had to develop the technique. We have talked about that at length in this book. But I also had to learn the management of the technique. That's what we'll talk about in the balance of this chapter.

As you read, try to separate style from substance. As a manager, I have my own style. It's fairly loose, upbeat, and with a good measure of theatrics thrown in. But beneath the style, there is substance. Perhaps the style makes the substance more palatable. But it is the substance that made it all work.

NOT THE COMPANY WAY

My first job in telephone marketing was with a little company that has long ceased to exist. Perhaps their training program had something to do with their disappearance.

It was all of an hour long. It consisted of a sales manager telling me, "Bill, here's the price list. There's your desk. That's the telephone. And here's where we keep all the Yellow Pages. Here is a copy of the script. If you have any questions, come and see me. You get paid every two weeks." I am sure there were a couple of other things thrown in, but this I can tell you for certain: After I was trained, I didn't know any more than when I started.

So I stood in my little office for a few moments, and then I went back to my manager. I asked him if it was okay if I didn't start making calls that day. "Steve," I said, "I'd like to listen to a few of the people around here before I get started and see if I can learn what they're doing. Who around here is making some money?"

Steve pointed to a man sitting not far from where my desk was. So I went over and introduced myself to him. He said his name was Don. I asked if it was all right if I spent an hour or two just listening to what he was doing. He said, "No problem."

So for two or three hours I listened to what Don said and did. I made a lot of notes. And it didn't take long to discover that what Don was doing was not the "official company way." Don had developed something quite different, and as I listened to him and wrote down what he was saying, I figured that instead of doing it the company way, I would do it Don's way. My assumption was that if I would just do what Don was doing I would probably make a lot of money.

That assumption was right on the money. As I got to work over the next few days, I shot past all of the other new salespeople. From my first teacher Don, I learned what may be the most important principle of all:

- **Find out what's working now and do that.**

IF IT WORKS, MAKE 'EM DO IT

After keeping my first job in telemarketing for about six months, I decided I should make a move into management. So I scouted around for a company where I might launch a "takeover." I found one with lot of empty space, a good product, a decent management, and no sales management. I began telling people how much money I was making and very quickly I got a flow of people coming in the door asking for jobs. All of a sudden, the general manager was flooded with people and was getting quite overworked. So I went to him, told him he had a problem, and suggested that he promote me to sales manager to solve the problem of what to do with all these people. He agreed. I had the job.

At this time, my new company was largely an order desk operation with a back-room telephone crew added on as an afterthought. As I recall, there were thirteen scruffy salespeople when I arrived. When I left about two and a half years later to start Telephone Marketing, there were over eighty in a brand new building that the owner had been forced to build in order to house this monster I created.

One of the early things I learned in my sales management career was actually taught to me by a young lady I had hired. Her name was Carey. As I began building my crew, I would write up various product descriptions and closes. With eighty to a hundred products, I soon had quite a pile of paper.

Carey was a promising saleswoman. But her production tended to fluctuate wildly week by week. I didn't know the cause, nor did she. One day as I passed her desk, I noticed her with a pile of 4 × 6 notecards, a pair of scissors, my product descriptions, and a pot of rubber cement. She was pasting the product descriptions and closes on cards.

I asked her, "Carey, what are you doing?"

She replied that she had noticed that whenever she stuck to the scripts, she made more money. But, she told me, "It's impossible to use all these scraps of paper you have written. So I'm pasting them up on some cue cards." I found that *very* interesting. So I kept a close eye on what she was doing.

Very shortly after getting her cue cards together, Carey's sales graph began to climb off the chart.

Up until this time, I had not really learned fully my lesson from Don. To be sure, I had learned it as a salesman. But I had not seen its full application as a manager. In my own sales, I would not consider ad libbing or winging a sales talk, but I had taken a laissez-faire attitude toward my salespeople and assumed that they would adapt what I had written to their style. Everyone, I thought, should have his or her own style.

Today, I know that idea to be rubbish, and it was really Carey that taught it to me.

Not long after her sales began their climb off the chart, I sat down in my office with cards, paper, rubber cement, and scissors and put together five sets of cue cards. I brought in five of my lower performing salespeople and told them that we had a new way of doing things. And for two or three hours I rehearsed them

211

on the cue cards and then sent them off to see what they could do. Without exception, their sales increased.

And before long, everyone but my top performers had their own set of cue cards. And sales went up substantially.

Don had taught me something very important as a salesman. Carey taught me something as a manager. Added together the principle became:

- **Find out what's working now and do that. Then get everyone who is not making enough money to do it also.**

To put it another way, I no longer believe a salesperson is entitled to do it his or her own way. As a manager, your job is to get people making money. So I would tell them:

- **If you're in the bottom eighty percent, you do it my way. Not until you're in the top twenty percent can you afford your own style.**

HOW TO STAY IN TOUCH WITH YOUR SALES CREW

To know if they're doing it your way, you have to stay in touch. You have to know what your top performers are doing, what your new people are doing, and even what your old mossback sluggards are doing. How else can you improve performance? And perhaps even more important, your crew has to know that you know and know that you care. Here's how I learned that lesson.

Very early, when there were fewer than twenty of us, it was no big deal for me to get around and talk to each person several times a day. I thus had a good feeling for who was doing well and who wasn't. And at the beginning of each week, I would sit down and make a list of all my salespeople, look at what they had done the previous week, estimate what they could do the current week, and set a goal for making more sales than the previous week.

But as we grew past twenty, there were too many people. I could not necessarily talk to each person each day, and that began to present a problem. My planning fell apart because I didn't know who was doing what and who needed what when.

So I established a daily report system. I decided on a daily report since by Friday the week is already gone and there is nothing you can do about it. I liked to know by the day, and in some cases by the hour, how people were doing.

So I came up with a simple form (similar to Chart 2 in Chapter 10), which each member of my crew would fill out daily. It was to be labeled Daily/Weekly Report and put in a basket on my desk. Each day I would review it and hand it back. At the end of the week, I would file it in the person's personnel folder. Everyone would cooperate and no problem. Right? (A sample copy of the form is shown on page 214.) Easier said than done.

It took me about six weeks of cajoling, threatening, cutting off sources of lead cards, and other uses of bribery and coercion to establish the habit that people were going to keep their statistics and turn them in to me daily.

Once I got them doing it, this simple Daily/Weekly Report became very important to me, and perhaps even more important to my sales crew. It enabled me to know where to spend my management time, and it served to alert me to problems before they became disasters. To my sales crew, it seemed to be a way of letting them know someone cared.

One week, for whatever reason, I got a bit lazy and didn't turn the reports back on time. There was a storm of protest. People came up to me and asked, "Didn't you see how I did yesterday?" And that question came from people who had done well and wanted me to know it and from those who did poorly and needed help. That was the last time I failed to turn back the reports.

Looking back, my Daily/Weekly Report was just one of many channels with which my crew and I delivered and received communication. Some were formal, such as the Daily/Weekly Report. But others were informal and were perhaps even more important than the formal channels. One of the most important channels was the simple act of handing out lead cards.

In my office I had a giant file cabinet that would hold probably twenty-five thousand prospect names printed on 3 × 5 cards. I had access to more than three-quarters of a million such names stored in our computer. One of my jobs as sales manager was to make certain that people had enough names to call but not so

DAILY / WEEKLY REPORT

NAME _____   WEEK ENDING _____

DAY	HOURS	DIALS	CONTACTS	CHERRIES	2ND CALLS	APPTS. SET
MON						
TUE						
WED						
THU						
FRI						
TOT						

COMMENTS:

many they could hoard and thereby deprive others of good prospects. So typically I would give out twenty-five to fifty cards at a time. With eighty people doing at least some cold calling all the time, there would be days I couldn't even leave my office for a break without someone shouting at me that, "Hey Bill, don't go yet. I need some more cards." As you can well imagine, it was very difficult to get other work done.

One day, I got the bright idea to take my big filing cabinet and move it to my secretary's office and let her give out the lead cards. So I got two or three big strapping guys, a dolly, and we moved the cabinet into her office. And the trek of salespeople wearing holes in the carpet to my office diverted to her office. At last I had some peace and could get some work done.

Just as I required all of my salespeople to post their commissions on a graph, I posted two graphs in my office, one on new accounts and the other on commissions. That week both graphs dropped. I didn't think too much about that because I was always able to get the graph up again. As a matter of fact, for one six-month period there were only two two-week periods where either graph dropped two weeks in a row. This was one of those times. The other was when I was out sick.

So I was beating my brains to figure out what I had changed that would cause those graphs to go down. I had the same number of salespeople. We were selling the same products. To the same types of companies. Using the same script. The number of calls made was in line. The only thing I could think of was that . . . I had moved the lead file into my secretary's office!

So I moved it back. Sales promptly went up. I concluded that the "lead line" where salespeople came to me personally to get new lead cards had been an important source of information on how they were doing. As they came into my office, I would read smiles, frowns, other subtle signs and quite frequently send one back with a tape recorder to make a tape of his calls. When I moved the lead file, that line fell out, and with it I lost a significant amount of "touch" with my sales force.

From then on, the lead file stayed with me.

The principle I gleaned from this experience was:

- **There should be as many channels of communication between salespeople and manager as possible. The informal channels are at least as important as the formal ones.**

CHECK THE WHITES OF THEIR EYES

There are four major problems that can wipe out otherwise good salespeople. I got on the trail of one of them in an effort to track down what I came to call the one bad day a week phenomenon. I noticed that most everyone in my sales crew would have one bad day a week—sometimes two. When I gave it a bit more thought, I realized that those bad days were costing me about twenty percent of my sales. So I began to try and find out why a person would have a bad day.

To find out, I did everything I could think of. When one of my salespeople would hit a bad day, I would put him or her on tape. I would sit in their offices with them. I would work on their list, their presentation, their sound, and all the other variables we have discussed in this book.

Some of these bad days disappeared, but there was a hard core I couldn't crack. One day I was sitting in my office talking to a chap who had had two bad days in a row. He sounded good, was making lots of calls, his list was fine, and in short, I didn't have a clue why he was having a bad day. As I looked at him, I noticed his eyes were a bit bloodshot so I asked him, "Mike, how much sleep did you get last night?"

"Plenty."

"That's not what I asked. What time did you go to bed?"

"About two o'clock."

"And what time did you get up?"

"About five-thirty."

"Mike, get out of here. And don't come back until you've had a good night's rest." And I threw him out.

The next day, he came back and I performed what later came to be called the white-of-the-eyes check. I grabbed him, jerked his head back, pulled his eyelids open, and he looked okay. I then asked him how much sleep he had had, and he said, "ten hours." I put him back on the phone, and he did fine.

Was I ever interested in this!

So I prowled around the sales halls looking for people not doing well. I found five. One of them I sorted out, and the other four got sent home for exhaustion. It took one of them two days to come back. They all did as well or better as they had been doing before the bad day.

Conclusion:

- **Lack of sleep kills salespeople. If you can't find any other explanation for a bad day, find out about sleep.**

There is another, perhaps related, phenomenon you should know about. In analyzing when sales occurred, I would find in many cases that thirty to forty percent would occur in the first hour of the day and the balance in the last five to six hours. Now that just didn't make a lot of sense to me. So in checking it over, I found that people were not taking breaks. So I simply made it a policy that you could take your breaks in one of two ways:

1) Take ten minutes every hour;

2) Take a break after the second sale. One of the best salesmen ever taught me this one. Very early in my own sales career, he took me aside and told me, "Bill, let me tell you how you can double your income. Whenever you make the first sale, don't put down the phone. Keep calling. You're hot then. Take your break after the second one. In many cases, sales come in pairs."

Truer words were never spoken and to this day, this is a principle I try to apply in my own sales. When I'm hot, I keep at it.

The objective is to have several "first hours" during the day.

- **Make certain your crew takes frequent breaks. Try to encourage them to stay on the phone just after they find a prospect, set an appointment, or close a sale. There's another one where that one came from.**

Here's another important point: Very early in my own selling career, I noticed that when I was hungry, I didn't seem to do as well. Evidently, actual physical hunger translates into a sound that prospects identify as a "hungry salesman." Rather than gorge on pizza and beer, I recommend that a salesperson eat something before spending a couple of hours on the phone, and then if you feel your energy level begin to drop, get a snack.

- **Don't let 'em prospect hungry. Keep the blood sugar up and avoid the "hungry salesman sound."**

Finally, one of the best killers of salespeople is domestic strife. I can't tell you how many salespeople I have seen go down the chute in the midst of quarrelsome bickering at home. My only solution to this is to get both warring parties into your office and negotiate a truce. I had one salesman whom I had nurtured and cultured and trained to prove I could train anyone. And then all of a sudden he and his young wife went at each other. I called them both in my office and when they were both seated I turned to my salesperson and told him, "Mike, you're fired." His face turned white, his wife drew her lips together, and I just sat there and shut up. She finally broke silence and asked, "Why?"

And I told them, "You guys are at each other's throat and it's got Mike so upset that he can't sell. And he's no use to me. So he's fired."

And I again shut up.

Finally, she said, "We'll stop fighting."

I replied, "That's what I hoped you'd say."

And so I pulled out an agreement I had already typed up and presented it to them for their signature. The agreement said that they would only fight beginning at 5:00 P.M. on Friday and end by 6:00 P.M. on Sunday and would not fight during the week. I told them if they didn't sign it and if his sales didn't recover, he was looking for a job. They signed the agreement and stopped the shooting. Mike's sales recovered quite well.

HIRING NEW SALESPEOPLE

In telemarketing, there is a notoriously high turnover. As far as I can tell, the reason for it is that people don't make the kind of money they're promised. So they leave and search elsewhere.

Turnover varies from industry to industry. I've heard that in the securities industry it's about thirty-five percent of new hires. I think that's probably low. In insurance it's well over fifty percent. In real estate it's probably over eighty percent. And so management is constantly faced with the need to recruit.

Early on in my sales management career I had the false idea that

I somehow had the ability to spot the people who could succeed and get rid of the ones who would fail. Once my boss told me to hire a friend of his. After I had interviewed him, I went back to my boss and told him I didn't want to hire him. I said, "The guy's been out of work for two years, is demoralized, and the only thing I see happening is that he's going to get in here and demoralize the rest of the crew. I don't want to hire him."

He said, "It's my place. Hire him." And so I did.

Within a matter of days, it was obvious he would be a screaming success. So I decided then and there that I didn't know how to detect in advance whether a person had the ability to do this job, and quite frankly I don't think anyone else does either. A lot of people, mostly shrinks, make a lot of money testing recruits to see if they are suited for sales. (This is the same bunch that turns mental cases loose on the streets to commit mass murder.) Frankly, I don't think they have a clue who can succeed and who cannot. They may be screening out as many successes as failures.

Make no mistake. This is a very real problem for sales management. In the securities industry, it may cost from twenty-five thousand to forty thousand dollars to train one recruit. And you certainly want to know whether that person has a reasonable chance for success.

To be sure, a person in many industries does have to have a certain intelligence level in order to comprehend a sometimes bewildering amount of technical material. Intelligence tests do seem to be able to test for this. But the ability to handle the rough and tumble and rejection of a prospecting and selling career cannot, to my knowledge, be adequately tested. I know too many examples of people who literally failed the test, had a branch manager go to bat for them, and then became wildly successful.

The test misses some X-factor. There is something the shrinks cannot test for.

So how do you decide to hire someone?

The solution I came to, and which I have been recommending for several years now, is what I call the audition. Why not give potential salespeople a chance to audition for the job? Give them a short training course and let them prospect for an established

219

PROSPECTING YOUR WAY TO SALES SUCCESS

salesperson. It does not follow that a person who can find new business can then close it. But it is certainly the case that if prospective salespersons *cannot* find new business, they cannot succeed in most sales careers unless assigned some kind of territory working with established accounts.

So, as part of your hiring procedure, you need at least enough time to train the prospective employee enough to prospect. Explain that you want them to have a chance to find out what the work is actually like and that if they don't succeed in this part of it, they won't succeed elsewhere. I would recommend you pay them for their time and at the end of their probationary period, you have a second interview and review what they think as well as let them know what you think of their success.

HOW TO KEEP THEM DOWN ON THE FARM (OR KEEP THE PHONES DIALING)

One important tool for managers is certainly exhortation. By this I mean the manager needs to constantly urge his or her sales force to keep the phones dialing. But after days, weeks, or months of exhortation, it gets old and tiresome. So here are two methods you can use that will supplement or replace the simple need for continuous cheerleading.

If you yourself have gathered a good supply of lists, you can use "the list test." You take fifty names from a list, go by one of your salesperson's desks, plop them on the desk, and say, "Fred, I want you to call these names, keep track of them, and let me know the results. It's a new list. Why don't you have the results in my office in a couple of hours? Thanks." And you walk away. Needless to say, Fred has to make the calls in order to do the test.

Or try the tape ploy: When you see one of your salespeople looking out the window with a far-off and glazed look, grab a tape recorder and a telephone mike and go over to the desk. (If you have one of the newer electronic phone systems that won't record on the usual little suction cup mikes you can get at Radio Shack, you will need to have your vendor come in and install a cord that will plug into a tape recorder. Then, when you want to tape a salesperson, you will need to move the phone around. This is no problem because new phone systems all use modular jacks.)

Start wiring up the phone and tell the salesperson you are a little bit concerned and that you'd like him or her to make a tape of the calls. Put a two-hour cassette on the tape and ask him or her to please bring it to your office when it's done. And then walk away. To make a tape, they've got to make the calls.

Some sales managers have figured out that you can use a tape recorder as a time clock. Let's say you've told several of your salespeople to come in to make calls at night and you have other engagements. Give each of them a two-hour tape, and tell them that you'd like the tape on your desk the next morning. You don't have to tell them, of course, that you're using this as a method to see if they do their work. Your point of view should be that you want to help them, and the only way you can do that is if you have a tape. But you also know, in your heart of hearts, that the real objective is to get them making the calls.

MAGIC

Some of the principles we've talked about so far would come under the heading of good management. They are really routine actions. And certainly a lot of routine actions can create a wonderful sales force.

But to create a legend, a place that's fun and exciting to work, well, you need something more than routine actions. You need some magic. What's magic? Theater perhaps. Games. Surprises. Toughness. You need constant elements of unpredictability inserted into the humdrumness of routine. And magic creates money.

Contests

You can really work some magic with a good contest. Let's face it. No matter what you say or preach, a certain monotony can set in for a sales force that must do repetitive actions (cold calling, for example) on a daily basis. The monotony can and will be offset

221

by success, but even so, it is important that the manager introduce change so as to control it. Certain things, of course, we don't want to change. So we better have change elsewhere.

Contests can be one of the best elements of controlled change, and it's for this reason that I have never really liked long ones. To be an effective change element, a contest cannot last long. When a contest goes on for long periods of time, it becomes part of the landscape. It is, therefore, no change. And unless the prize is substantial, a contest really doesn't offer much incentive to do something that you would not do anyway. A contest, then, can just cost money instead of make money.

Short-term contests can definitely sweeten things up, however. For maximum effectiveness, the prize should generally not be cash but still something your people want. Every salesperson knows that if he or she gets just some extra money, taxes will get a bite and the rest of it will go to pay the overdue utility bill. And so he or she really doesn't have anything extra. Cash, interestingly, does not provide the best motivation available.

So how do you find out what they want? Simple. Ask. One time my old boss, who was as tight-fisted as they come, told me I could have two hundred dollars to spend on a prize. Big deal. I gave a lot of thought to what prize to offer, and when I didn't come up with anything that really rang my bell, I sent out a memo to all my salespeople asking them to write down a prize they'd like to have that cost in the range of two hundred dollars.

Lots of answers came back, and I went through them all and wrote down any answer that was mentioned more than once. There were six or eight of them. On another memo, I asked my crew to vote on which of those items they would most like to have as a prize.

When I tabulated their answers, the one that came out on top was a racing bicycle. It was a prize I would have never have guessed. But it seemed to be what the people wanted. So I bought one, put it in the salesroom, and announced the contest. I then witnessed one of the most amazing phenomenon I have ever seen. After a while, the contest was down to just a few people. They were working more hours, coming in earlier, staying later, messing around less. Some were making far more money than they ever had before, and any one of them could certainly have bought the blasted bicycle with their increased earnings. Winning may not be everything, but it was certainly the only thing that counted for this bunch. As we rolled into the last week, it was a slug fest. Some people were working twelve to fourteen hours a day to win the bike.

Certainly, part of the magic of contests is the prize. But the other part seems to be the possibility of winning. To make certain I got as many players as possible, I handicapped my top performers by making everyone compete against his or her own previous best effort. This gave the new kids on the block a chance to make a run at the old kids. And it was a new kid who took the prize.

THE FIRST MAGIC PRINCIPLE:

- **You can buy a lot of sales for a little money if everyone gets a chance to win and if you offer something that people really want.**

Magic Cards

Very soon after I took over as sales manager, I put a box by the door to my office so salespeople could throw in lead cards they didn't want. Before long it became known as the junk card box. Every once in a while I would go through it, sort it out, and give them out again. No one ever knew the difference.

One day, for no apparent reason, I got an idea. I wanted to see if I could turn junk cards into "magic cards." So I closed the door to my office, dumped the cards out on the floor, sorted through them, and pulled out certain types of cards in certain geographical areas that I felt were probably okay.

I then took those cards, put them in a file box that had a lock on it, and put the box on my desk. I took a black marker, and I wrote the words "Magic Cards" on the file box and just left it sitting on my desk.

It was actually a few days before someone asked, "Bill, what on earth are those?"

My reply was, "Don't you touch my cards. They're my solution to you. If you all decide to fail in this business, I'll take that box of cards and go and make some money with it. As a matter of fact,

223

you shouldn't even be allowed to be in the same room with these cards. They are magic. Now get out of here."

Needless to say, he went out immediately to the other salespeople and told them I had slipped mentally again. Before long, someone else came in the office on some pretext or other and made some crack about the magic cards. I threw him out as well. Over the next two or three days several people made unkind comments. I just smiled and would grab the box and stuff it in the drawer and make a big show of throwing them out of the office since they had mentioned my magic cards in an unpleasant manner.

After I let this run for several days, I was having a talk with one of my salespeople who was having a bad day. All of a sudden I looked over at him and asked, "Tom, would you like to try some of my magic cards?"

He brightened up and said yes.

"All right," I said, "Down on your knees and beg." And I made him beg for some magic cards. While he was still down on his knees I very carefully counted out twenty-five cards, made him put his hands on the cards and close his eyes. I then proceeded to bless the cards. I asked him, "All the bad vibes gone?" "Oh, yes," he replied.

"All right," I said, "Get the hell out of here and go make some sales."

He came back in fifteen minutes or so with a great big smile on his face and said, "It worked!" He showed me the order he had just written.

And so the parade started. Everyone wanted some magic cards. But I would only give them out maybe once or twice a day to someone who was having some serious problems. And usually they worked.

All of which brings us now to the definition of a "great list."

- **A great list is simply a good list in which people believe. And belief must be created and sustained by the manager.**

Certainly I am not the only one to have identified this principle. I have never seen it written anywhere, but many good sales managers have grasped it almost instinctively.

One of my very good friends in the brokerage industry, Hank Merrill, former training director of Paine Webber, had this idea down cold. When he was a branch manager in Milwaukee, he used to hire high school girls to come into the office on Saturday mornings. They would copy down names and phone numbers onto note cards from the street address directory. During the week, when brokers would be having a bad day, they would come and ask for some of Hank's "special lists." Everyone agreed that his cards were much better than the street address directory. He was often accused of using the street address directory as his source but he would never confess to where the names came from. He just told everyone that if he let them know where the names came from, everyone would go and get them and he would lose control of his source.

THE SECOND MAGIC PRINCIPLE:

- **Actions that build belief are magic.**

If you wish people to believe something is valuable, act as if it is. I know one branch manager who keeps his list locked in a big file cabinet with a steel reenforcing bar bolted to the cabinet.

The Magic Tape Recorder

I forget exactly when I discovered the principle of the magic tape recorder. Nor do I recall who my guinea pig was, but I recall very distinctly telling someone to make me a tape of his calls, and then having him run right back in and tell me he just got a sale.

That happened a few more times. So I went out and bought five tape recorders and whenever anyone was having a bad day, I would have them make a tape. In many cases I would never even listen to the tape because once they started making the tape, they would quit doing things that they had been doing and do it the correct way—my way!

For the magic tape recorder to work, you first must have a prospecting and sales method that works. You also need to have demonstrated that you will crawl down the throat of salespeople who depart from the successful method. Given those two ingredients, when someone is having a bad day you simply tell them to make a tape. And they'll quit doing those things that they know you'll crawl down their throat for and start doing them correctly. And after a while, especially if you make a few comments about your magic tape recorders, your crew will make remarks about your sanity. But when they're not doing well, they'll come and ask if they can borrow your recorder. And they'll do this even if they have one of their own right in their office.

THE THIRD MAGIC PRINCIPLE:

- **A little magic goes a long way.**

The Magic of Average

Nobody wants to be average. Not even the people who are. Or those who are below average. But there is some magic in "the average" that a sales manager can use to raise it. Here's how it works:

A few weeks after I was appointed sales manager, I asked the computer operator to give me a production run of my salespeople's previous couple of months. As I studied it, I realized it was quite a miserable, scruffy bunch. The average person working there was making about $175 a week. When I divided that by five and did a little rounding, I concluded that the average salesperson was making less than $35 a day. Without giving it much thought, I decided that anyone making less than that was in serious need of retraining. My average became the minimum acceptable. So I announced that anyone who made less than $35 on any given day would attend an obligatory meeting the next day at 9:45 in the morning. And that was that. No questions about it. This later became known as the bornyak meeting. I came to define a "bornyak" as the lowest form of human life known that had only recently been discovered because it had such a short life expectancy. And lo and behold, there were some bornyaks working for me and they could be identified because they made less than $35 a day and were in danger of imminent starvation.

In their efforts to avoid the stigma of being called bornyaks and being forced to attend a bornyak meeting, those below average began to achieve the minimum. And arithmetically, of course, the average shot up.

Every manager knows that salespeople need individual goals to achieve. Very few know how to help the salesperson set the goal. It's absolutely senseless to speak to someone about "shooting for a goal of three thousand dollars a week" if the most he or she has ever made is twelve thousand a year. You might as well talk about eliminating the national debt.

To be achievable, a goal has to be real. And it is my belief that to those below average the average of the group *is very real*. And so in my first efforts at goal setting, I happened upon a highly successful formula that was to set a *minimum* for those below average to achieve. And that minimum was the average of the group.

What about those above average? Take the production of the above average group and average it. The new minimum acceptable for this group is roughly twenty-five percent higher than the average for those below. And so on with your top twenty-five percent. The two or three salespeople on top are given a *minimum* of their previous best efforts. As each works to achieve the minimum, you'll see the average of the entire group go up dramatically. And, presto chango, you have an entirely new set of minimums. It's magic.

THE FOURTH MAGIC PRINCIPLE:

- **Give the individual members of a group a minimum acceptable level. Hold a torch under them, and then get out of the way.**

Building Stars

I once hired a young man I didn't really want to hire. He kept coming around pestering me for a job, and so I finally decided to let him have a try at it just to get him off my back. He was sensational. I made a tape of his calls one day, just for my own education, and shortly thereafter, a new trainee asked me if he could listen to someone. So I gave him "Bill Loman's" tape. (My new salesman had a last name that was fairly hard to pronounce and decided to invent his own name. In a flash of inspiration, he first called himself Willy Loman, after the character in *Death of a Salesman*. Too many people were familiar with that, and he changed it to Bill Loman. Throughout tens of thousands of calls, only one person, to my knowledge, ever called him on it.)

At any rate, when the new person had listened to Bill's tape and heard him rack up several hundred dollars in commissions in just a few calls, he was, necessarily, excited about coming to work. So I got him signed up and started on his training. Later that afternoon, he came up to me and he pointed to someone in the hall and said, "Is that Bill Loman?" I said it was, and took him over and introduced him.

There was a little magic that happened there. Bill was more than flattered, and my new salesperson was in awe. And over a period of many months thereafter, the Bill Loman tape was a very important part of my training program. Not only did it serve to train the new people, but it gave me a tool to constantly enhance and reinforce the "great salesman image" that Bill quite rightly deserved.

Yes, rewards and plaques and trips and special badges and corner offices are all important to the sometimes all-too-fragile ego of salespeople. However, if you really want to help build a solid self-image for a salesperson, deliberately use your better salespeople as role models for your up-and-comers.

THE FIFTH MAGIC PRINCIPLE:

- **Once held up as a role model and preserved on audio or video cassette, no salesperson will ever fall back to a point where the honor is no longer deserved.**

The Magic of Product Knowledge

The question about product knowledge is: How much is enough? This really brings us to the question: Why do you need to know?

In my experience, salespeople need product training primarily for one reason: to build belief and certainty that the product is good. If the salesperson believes in the product, and if he or she also knows enough to know whether a particular product will solve the problem the customer has, he or she really doesn't need to know very much more. But they do need to *believe*.

Let me give a very simple example. One of my very first clients was a company that sold central air conditioning to homeowners. It was a pretty hard-sell outfit and has since gone by the boards. My job was to work with and train the soliciting crew that set the appointments for the salespeople. The sales manager had a hard-and-fast rule that you didn't teach salespeople about product. He was afraid they would get into conversations about air conditioners. All he wanted them to do was set appointments. Some of them didn't even know what they were setting the appointment for.

So I convinced him to let two or three of his best salespeople come in and give product demonstrations to the soliciting crew. One of the products this particular company offered was an electrostatic air purifier. They had developed a pretty dramatic demonstration for it by enclosing the thing in a Plexiglas box. Someone would light a cigarette, blow smoke into the Plexiglas box, flip on the electrostatic purifier, and the smoke would disappear in an instant. It happened to be a very good product, and was especially suited for people who had allergies to air-borne particles.

When the soliciting crew saw the demonstration, it was as if magic had been done. They got excited. They wanted to see it again. And no sooner were they back on the phone than they were hammering away to discover if people had any allergy-related problems or any other problem for which the air purifier would be a solution. In the next few weeks, more electrostatic air purifiers were sold than in the previous few months. And it was done for one reason only: The salespeople believed in the product. And yet, how many product coordinators or product trainers make the presentation of the product as dull as a bucket of old mud water!

THE SIXTH MAGIC PRINCIPLE:

- **Get a crack salesperson who believes in the product to teach it. Have them demonstrate it as if they're trying to sell it.**

BUILDING LOYALTY

While it's true that any sales manager is motivated, at least in part, by his or her own desire to make money, it certainly helps if you are motivated by a genuine desire to help others live better.

It is the ability actually to help people improve their lot in life that creates a tremendous loyalty among salespeople for a manager. I remember very well a young man named Mike. He was nineteen years old and had a terrible voice—he sounded as if he were speaking through a three-foot-nose. He also had a seventeen-year-old, equally frightened, pregnant wife. (It was Mike I mentioned earlier whom I had forced to sign the agreement that he wouldn't fight with his wife.)

I hired him for two reasons. Number one, he really wanted and needed the job. And number two, I guess I wanted to prove to myself that I could train anyone, and he was as good a representative of "anyone" as I expected to find.

For weeks I invested a lot more of my time in him than one would have thought he was worth, but finally he began to come around. His sales began creeping up. And over the next several months, he got up to where he was making $300 to $400 a week, which for those times, and especially for him, was not all that bad. He was at least surviving.

Though it is many years after that, I believe that to this day I could call Mike up and tell him, "Mike, I want you to go stand down on the end of the Venice Pier and wait for a little green man. I don't have time to explain right now but I'll call you back later." *Click, dial tone.*

Now Mike might think that I had fused a circuit board, but he would know that at the bottom of everything, he owes me one. I picked him up when he was down and helped him survive better.

Good managers really can do that. In reality, most of the salespeople you hire will have been failures somewhere else. Had they not failed elsewhere, perhaps even high-level failure, they probably wouldn't be knocking on your door. And it is out of

230

these failures that a great manager can build spectacular successes.

My hope for you as a manager is that you will help. Sales can be a wonderful and rewarding career. With help, many more can succeed than do.

Thankyouverymuch.

For Further Improvement in Prospecting and Sales

To improve your overall prospecting skills, the following items are available from Bill Good at Telephone Marketing, Inc.

The Good Way to Prospect—a cassette album on prospecting by Bill Good

Cherries and Pits: A One-Day Prospecting Seminar.

For details on cassettes, seminars, or other services, call or write to:

TELEPHONE MARKETING, INC.
870 East 9400 South
Sandy, Utah 84070
(801) 572-1480

For help in improving your lists, you may want to own these two books (they are also available in most libraries):

Encyclopedia of Associations: National Organizations of the U.S., Vol. 1. Ed. by Denise Akey. Gale Research Co., Detroit, MI, 1984.

Directory of Directories, 3rd ed. Ed. by James M. Ethridge. Gale Research Co., Detroit, MI, 1984.

To improve your sales ability:

How I Raised Myself from Failure to Success in Selling by Frank Bettger, Prentice-Hall Inc., Englewood Cliffs, NJ, 1983.

To get organized and improve your work habits:

The Problems of Work: How to Solve Them & Succeed by L. Ron Hubbard. Bridge Publications, Inc., Los Angeles, CA, 1983.

For a better understanding of marketing:

POSITIONING: The Battle for your Mind by Al Ries and Jack Trout. Warner Books Inc., New York, 1982.

Marketing Warfare by Al Ries and Jack Trout. McGraw-Hill, New York, 1986.

Index

237

About the Author

Bill Good is president of Telephone Marketing, Inc., a firm specializing in helping salespeople find new business by phone.

Bill and the staff at Telephone Marketing, Inc. have designed prospecting systems for companies in the insurance industry, residential real estate, telecommunications, commercial real estate, and, of course, for the stock brokerage industry. Bill's monthly column, Successful Prospecting, is one of the most popular features in *Registered Representative,* the major trade magazine for the securities industry. Bill and his staff have delivered over a thousand seminars in the industry to all the national firms as well as most regional and local firms.

Before founding Telephone Marketing, Inc. in November of 1977, Bill was sales manager for the largest telephone sales company in California. He built it from thirteen sales people to over eighty in less than two years and set expansion records that have never been touched since.

When he opened Telephone Marketing, he had saved the grand total of $1000 and had two clients. As he puts it, I "hit the ground running." By 1980, he had trained over five thousand insurance agents, one thousand real estate agents, and numerous salespeople from dozens of other industries. As real estate fell on hard times in 1979–80, Bill switched over to the securities industry, and by 1984, he was invited to become a keynote speaker for the Securities Industry Association annual meeting in 1984.

Bill lives in Sandy, Utah, with his wife Joava and his two daughters, Nicci and Jenny. Rumor has it that he is tired of the cold and that if anyone wants to buy a lovely home with a beautiful view of the mountains, they should give him a call.

Bill welcomes letters from readers and promises to do his best to answer them promptly. You can write to him at the address below, and even though he may be long gone to warmer places, all mail will be forwarded to him.

Bill Good
9710 S. 700 East Suite 102
Sandy, Utah 84070